Suicide

PREVENTION IN CUSTODY

Self-Instructional Course

FOUNDED 1870
American Correctional Association

a publication of the
AMERICAN CORRECTIONAL ASSOCIATION
4380 Forbes Boulevard
Lanham, MD 20706-4322
(301) 918-1800
Fax: (301) 918-1900
http://www.corrections.com/ACA

ISBN 1-56991-062-6

Acknowledgments

Developing a correspondence course requires the efforts of many individuals. We would like to acknowledge and thank those professionals who created and reviewed *Suicide Prevention in Custody.*

Author

Joseph R. Rowan*
Executive Director and Chair
Criminal and Juvenile Justice International, Inc.
Roseville, MN

* who wrote the manuscript and devoted many hours to the production of the course

Review Committee

External

Gary L. Dennis, Ph.D.
Director of Mental Health
Kentucky Department of Corrections
Frankfort, KY

Deborah L. Graves
Training Development Specialist Senior
Department of Juvenile Justice Staff Training
Louisville, KY

Carlyn Schlossberg
Psychologist Associate II—Corrections
Maryland Correctional Institution—Jessup
Jessup, MD

Sam S. Whitted
Chief Deputy
Coconino County Sheriff's Department
Flagstaff, AZ

Linda Young-Miller, Ph.D.
Staff Psychologist
Federal Correctional Institution
Dublin, CA

Internal

John J. Greene, III
Director
Professional Development
American Correctional Association

Robert B. Levinson, Ph.D.
Special Projects Manager
American Correctional Association

Foreword

The American Correctional Association is pleased to offer the revised edition of the *Suicide Prevention in Custody Self-Instructional Course*. The course has benefitted thousands of correctional staff since its initial publication. The second edition has been extensively revised and updated by renowned author Joseph R. Rowan, who has over 50 years of experience in criminal and juvenile justice—not only nationally but also in over a dozen foreign countries.

Suicides in custody usually occur more frequently than they do in the community. In the correctional setting, suicide is both an ethical issue, and a legal issue. Correctional staff are responsible for the care and custody of offenders. When an offender commits suicide, the incident can tear apart a facility emotionally—even when things were done right and according to proper procedures. Regardless of the circumstances surrounding a suicide, the offender's family often questions the care given to their loved one and files a lawsuit. The staff and the facility then may be under the media spotlight.

Fortunately, well-trained staff can prevent most suicides in custody. We designed *Suicide Prevention in Custody* to help you prevent the tragedy of suicide from occurring in your facility.

Departments of corrections or individual facilities can incorporate this course into their pre-service and in-service training programs. In addition, the self-instructional format of this course allows correctional personnel to study during their free time and work at their own pace. By completing this course and others like it, correctional officers can increase their chances for promotion.

On behalf of the American Correctional Association, we wish you a successful career in corrections. Please write and tell us about your career and give us feedback on this edition of our course.

James A. Gondles, Jr.
Executive Director

How to Study This Course

This course has been designed to be used by you without the assistance or supervision of an instructor. The most effective way to study the material is:

- First, read the text. By carefully studying the information you are given, you should be able to understand the key points. You may want to highlight the portions of the text that seem particularly important. This is also a good way to review the materials later.

- At the end of each section of text, you will find a set of questions designed to see how well you have read and understood the material presented. These questions may require you to select an answer from a list of possible choices, or may ask you to write out a short response. Whatever the format of the question, read it carefully and select the best answer. You may want to review the text to help you select the best answer.

- After responding to each question, check your answer against the answer key located at the end of each chapter. Each question has a number printed next to it which corresponds to the correct response in the answer key. The question numbers are scrambled, so there is no advantage in looking at the next answer while you are checking the first one. If you miss a question, go back to the text and try to figure out why a different response was correct.

Read the sample question below and mark the best answer. The question is number 5. Check your answer in the answer key at the end of the first chapter in this course, "The Impact, Rate, and Prevention of Suicides."

QUESTIONS

Put a check (✓) by the right answer. The focus of this course is:

_____ A. Food service

_____ B. Correctional industries

_____ C. Suicide prevention

_____ D. Anger management

How to Study This Course (continued)

Number 5 in the answer key at the end of the first chapter reads:

The focus of this course is:

_____   A.   Food service

_____   B.   Correctional industries

✓   C.   Suicide prevention

_____   D.   Anger management

If you marked C, you are correct. If you did not get the answer right, mark the correct answer in your book and re-read the text. Find out where you made your mistake. Sometimes, the answer key will give you more information about why some answers are correct and others are not.

You should find working through the course exciting and rewarding. You will receive a certificate from the American Correctional Association upon successfully completing the final test. Good luck!

Table of Contents

Suicide Prevention in Custody—Self-Instructional Course

Table of Contents (continued)

NOTE: We developed this course primarily for the direct service workers (correctional officers, juvenile careworkers, admissions/intake workers, and classification workers) who work with adult and juvenile offenders, but it also would be beneficial for supervisors and administrators.

Throughout the course, we use the term "correctional worker" instead of the cumbersome correctional officer/juvenile careworker. Also, we use the term "offender" instead of the cumbersome "inmate/juvenile." In addition, we primarily use the term "he" instead of the cumbersome "he/she."

The Impact, Rate, and Prevention of Suicides

Objectives

At the end of this chapter, you will be able to:

1. Name at least three levels or types of personnel commonly named in suicide-related lawsuits.

2. Explain the extent of suicides in correctional facilities nationwide.

3. List at least six factors that help prevent suicide attempts and completed suicides.

Introduction

Someone once said that suicide is a "permanent solution to a temporary problem." In the correctional setting, suicide is both a moral or ethical issue, and a legal issue. Offenders are placed in the care and custody of correctional facilities. When an offender commits suicide, the incident can have a tremendous impact on staff, offenders, and their families. Indeed, suicides can tear apart a facility emotionally—even when "everything was done right" and according to proper procedures.

Suicidal behavior is costly not only in terms of human lives but also in dollars and cents. Family members often will question the care given to their loved ones and file suicide-related lawsuits. Thus, the costs for legal defense can be burdensome to a facility.

Fortunately, most suicides in custody can be prevented.

This chapter will discuss the impact and rate of suicides in custody, and review the key factors in preventing suicides.

The Impact of Suicide

The single incident feared most by administrators and staff in a detention or correctional facility—with the possible exception of a riot—is an unnatural death. Deaths by suicide, homicide, and undiagnosed medical conditions often cause severe stress among both staff and offenders. Frequently, these deaths place the facility under the spotlight of public criticism.

Even when they have followed recognized policies and procedures, staff often have strong guilt feelings after a suicide. They will ask, "What could we have done to prevent the suicide?"

Regardless of the circumstances surrounding an unnatural death, the media and offender advocacy groups will sometimes question whether reasonable care (defined by law as "duty of care") was provided. In recent years, relatives of offenders who have committed suicide have filed an increasing number of lawsuits. Liability often has been assessed to financing bodies (e.g., a city council), administrators, supervisors, and direct care staff for failure to carry out a reasonable duty of care in preventing suicides.

Included in the direct care group are an increasing number of contractual staff and medical and mental health workers. They too have been found liable for failing to follow reasonable standards and recognized practices in identifying and managing suicidal people.

Governmental agencies must monitor and hold contractual staff accountable, as if they were their own staff. Otherwise, the agency can be held liable.

Correctional staff (facility or contractual) may be surprised when they're named in a lawsuit because their last contact with the inmate who committed suicide was some time ago. Despite the passage of time, however, they still may be held liable for failure to provide reasonable care. For example, they may have taken a poor or inadequate history at admission (intake or booking). Or, they may not have reported or documented suicide risk behaviors, which you will learn about in this course. Each jurisdiction has a statute of limitations or time period by which a lawsuit must be filed.

Q

QUESTIONS

In recent years, suicide-related lawsuits have been filed against:

• _____

• _____

• _____

(3)

True/False   The only staff who may be held liable in a suicide-related lawsuit are those who have had recent contact with the offender who committed suicide.

(6)

The Rate of Suicides in Custody

Studies have shown that suicides in custody usually occur two to nine times more frequently than suicides in the community.

Natural causes of death, including AIDS, now exceed urban jail suicides. In urban area jails, AIDS deaths outnumber suicides by 40 percent. But suicide is the number one cause of unnatural death in medium and small-size jails (adult local detention facilities).

In fact, suicide occurs over five times more frequently in jails than in prisons. Those serving sentences in state and federal prisons generally have a lower suicide rate for several reasons. By the time they enter prison, offenders are not under the influence of alcohol or drugs; in contrast, about 60 percent of the offenders who are admitted to jails are intoxicated or high. Further, those in prison already may have survived the shock of incarceration and received attention for their emotional and mental problems.

In juvenile facilities, homicides occur twice as often as suicides. But suicide is the second leading cause of death. Suicides among male juveniles have increased noticeably in recent years, following an up-and-down pattern over several years.

Factors influencing the recent alarming increase in juvenile suicides and homicides in communities nationwide are the same that affect juvenile suicides and homicides in custody.

These factors include:

- Feelings of hopelessness about the future
- Problems in the family
- High rate of violence in movies and television

The rate of suicides by juveniles in adult jails is approximately eight times greater than that in juvenile detention facilities. Therefore, you must consider all juveniles in adult jails as high suicide risks.

Note: The Juvenile Justice and Delinquency Prevention Act of 1974 clearly states that adult and juvenile offenders must be separated by sight and sound while in custody. The above statistic adds further justification for removing juveniles from adult jails.

QUESTIONS

True/False   Jails and prisons have a lower rate of suicide than that in the community.

(1)

True/False   Juveniles in adult jails are high suicide risks.

(4)

5

CHAPTER 1
The Impact, Rate, and
Prevention of Suicides

Suicides Can Be Prevented

Many lawsuits have revealed that both officers and mental health staff have negative attitudes toward certain offenders. Sometimes, staff manage offenders as "manipulators" (those who are trying to "beat the system" and, thus, should be ignored) rather than as potentially suicidal. In some cases, staff are unable to control their feelings about the heinous crimes that the offenders committed. These negative attitudes often lead to neglectful behavior that fosters completed suicides—deaths which might otherwise have been prevented.

By following recognized policies, procedures, and practices, staff can prevent most suicides in custody. Statistics from both adult and juvenile detention and correctional facilities have demonstrated this fact. The most dramatic reduction in suicides, nearly 90 percent, occurred in over 300 county and city jails/lockups in New York State from 1984 to 1993.

Cook County Jail, Chicago, reduced suicides by nearly 80 percent from 1980 to 1993, while the average daily population skyrocketed from 3,700 to nearly 10,000 offenders.

Human interaction and good interpersonal communication are the most important aspects of suicide prevention. This means following the Golden Rule: *treating others as you want to be treated.*

Other key factors in suicide prevention are at least six to eight hours of basic training on identifying suicidal behavior and managing potentially suicidal behavior; periodic refresher training; screening offenders at admission; continuously assessing offenders for suicide risk; constant or close monitoring of suicidal offenders; good communication among staff; and proper housing for all offenders.

Q

QUESTIONS

List the two most important aspects of suicide prevention.

• _____

• _____

(2)

List three additional key factors in preventing suicides.

• _____

• _____

• _____

(7)

This chapter discussed the impact and rate of suicides in custody, and reviewed the key factors in preventing suicides.

1. Name at least three levels or types of personnel commonly named in suicide-related lawsuits.

   - In recent years, relatives of offenders who have committed suicide have filed an increasing number of lawsuits.

   - Liability often has been assessed to financing bodies, administrators, supervisors, and direct care staff for failure to carry out a reasonable duty of care in preventing suicides.

2. Explain the extent of suicides in correctional facilities nationwide.

   - The rate of suicides in custody usually far exceeds that in the community.

   - Suicide is the number two cause of death in juvenile correctional and detention facilities.

   - Suicide is the number one cause of unnatural deaths in small and medium-size jails.

3. List at least six factors that help prevent suicide attempts and completed suicides.

   - By following recognized policies, procedures, and practices, staff can prevent most suicides in custody. Statistics from both adult and juvenile detention and correctional facilities have demonstrated this fact.

   - The most important aspects of suicide prevention are human interaction and good interpersonal communication. This means following the Golden Rule: *treating others as you want to be treated.*

   - Other key factors in suicide prevention are at least six to eight hours of basic training on identifying suicidal behavior and managing potentially suicidal behavior; periodic refresher training; screening offenders at admission; continuously assessing offenders for suicide risk; constant or close monitoring of suicidal offenders; good communication among staff; and proper housing for all offenders.

Answer Key—The Impact, Rate, and Prevention of Suicides

1. **False.** Jails and prisons have a **higher** rate of suicide than that in the community.

2. The most important aspects of suicide prevention are:

    • Human interaction

    • Good interpersonal communication

3. In recent years, suicide-related lawsuits have been filed against: (choose three)

    • Correctional workers

    • Administrators

    • Financing bodies

    • Medical and mental health workers

    • Supervisors

4. **True.** Juveniles in adult jails are high suicide risks.

5. The focus of this course is:
    - _____ A. Food service
    - _____ B. Correctional industries
    - ✓ C. Suicide prevention
    - _____ D. Anger management

6. **False.** Any staff member who had contact with the offender who committed suicide may be held liable in a suicide-related lawsuit—regardless of the passage of time.

7. Additional key factors in preventing suicides are: (choose three)

    • At least six to eight hours of basic training on identifying suicidal behavior and managing potentially suicidal behavior

    • Periodic refresher training

    • Screening offenders at admission

    • Continuously assessing offenders for suicide risk

    • Constant or close monitoring of suicidal offenders

    • Good communication among staff

    • Proper housing for all offenders

CHAPTER TWO

Research on Suicides in Custody

Objectives

At the end of this chapter, you will be able to:

1. List at least two factors that make it difficult to obtain statistics on suicides in custody.

2. Identify the various levels of suicide risk by type of facility.

3. Define the term "suicide profile" and identify the type that is the most reliable.

4. List at least six traits that are considered to be major "red flags" for potentially suicidal behavior.

5. List four important predictors of potentially suicidal behavior.

Introduction

You learned in Chapter 1 that suicides in custody are a major problem for all correctional staff. The reported suicide rate in custody usually ranges from two to nine times the rate in the community. Many factors make it difficult to obtain accurate suicide statistics. Even studies focusing on the same type of offenders in different parts of the country reveal different statistics.

Why are these statistics important to you? They will help you understand the type of offenders in your facility that are most likely to commit suicide. Statistics will not help you identify all suicidal offenders. However, they are a critical factor in preventing suicides.

This chapter will identify the reasons for the difficulty in obtaining reliable statistics. It will discuss the statistical risks for suicides among various types of offenders. It also will cite cautions you should exercise when using a suicide profile (a list of traits identified in persons who have committed suicide).

Why the Difficulty in Obtaining Accurate Suicide Statistics?

Several situations cloud the reporting of suicides in both the community and in custody. Medical examiners or coroners may report suicides as "natural deaths" or "unknown causes of death." The examiners write such reports to save embarrassment to families and/or to protect families from losing insurance payments (because many insurance policies have clauses excluding from coverage individuals who commit suicide).

Legally, in some states, only a physician or other qualified* health personnel can pronounce a person dead. The offender may be dead long before he is discovered but death is pronounced at the hospital. Thus, it is often not counted as an institution death.

In addition, research about suicides in custody reveals that sometimes officials simply fail to report suicides. For example, a city police department lockup had six suicides within 18 months. The local newspaper, however, didn't report a single one. The facility didn't report the suicides or, perhaps, the newspaper itself decided not to publish them.

> Research about suicides in custody reveals that sometimes officials simply fail to report suicides.

QUESTIONS

Various factors influence statistics on suicides in custody. They include:

____ A. Saving embarrassment to families

____ B. Protecting families from losing insurance payments

____ C. Allowing only a physician or other qualified health personnel to pronounce a person dead

____ D. All of the above

(1)

True/False   It is difficult to obtain accurate statistics on suicides in custody.

(5)

Qualified health personnel are licensed, registered, and/or certified.

Suicide Risk Varies Among Offenders

The risk for suicide differs among offenders, depending upon whether they are adult or juvenile and whether they are in short-term (jail/detention) or long-term (prison/training school) facilities.

Male offenders commit over 90 percent of all suicides in custody.

Both juvenile and adult offenders have a higher risk for suicide in short-term facilities than in long-term facilities. Moreover, juveniles placed in adult jails commit suicide almost eight times more often than they do in separate juvenile detention facilities. One reason this occurs stems from the requirement for sight and sound separation from adults. Staff time and programs are provided more generously for the majority of offenders—adult—while the one or two juvenile detainees have fewer programs, are in isolation, and have little contact with staff. Thus, the juveniles may experience sensory deprivation and depression, which can lead to suicidal behavior.

In all facilities, idleness, boredom, inadequate monitoring, and harsh emotional and physical conditions influence the suicide rate.

Q

QUESTIONS

Offenders in _____ facilities present a higher statistical risk for suicide than offenders in _____ facilities.

(6)

Juveniles in _____ commit suicide almost eight times more often than they do in_____.

(10)

True/False Juveniles in adult jails are subjected to isolation more frequently than adults, a serious factor that increases the suicide rate.

(15)

Suicide Risk Varies Among Offenders (continued)

Pre-trial detainees in police lockups and detention facilities or jails have the highest rate of suicides. Arrestees entering these facilities are high-risk suicide candidates because:

- A high percentage of them are under the influence of alcohol and/or street drugs when they are arrested.

- Many are experiencing the trauma of arrest and incarceration for the first time.

- Many have a history of mental, emotional, social, and economic problems.

QUESTIONS

The highest rate of suicides occurs among:

_____ A. Parolees

_____ B. Pre-trial detainees

_____ C. Convicted offenders

_____ D. Probationers

(2)

Facilities with the highest suicide rate are:

_____ A. Lockups

_____ B. Prisons

_____ C. Detention facilities

_____ D. Both 1 and 3

(7)

Over 90 percent of all suicides in custody are committed by _____ offenders.

(16)

The suicide rate is greater for adult pre-trial detainees than for juvenile pre-trial detainees in separate juvenile detention facilities because:

- Adults generally have a longer history of alcohol, drug, and mental health problems.

- Staffing in juvenile detention facilities is generally more adequate than in jails.

- There is often less idleness in juvenile detention facilities than in jails.

- The control factor usually is more severe in jails than in juvenile detention facilities. Thus, the "caring attitude" is often greater in juvenile detention facilities than in jails.

- Juveniles are not kept as long in detention awaiting final disposition as adults are.

The above factors far outweigh the fact that juveniles are more immature and impulsive—a significant factor contributing to suicide.

Sentenced/adjudicated offenders in state and local prisons, and training schools/treatment facilities have a lower suicide rate than pre-trial detainees because:

- They almost always enter the prison/ detention facility in a sober and a detoxified condition.

- They already have survived the trauma of incarceration in the lockup and detention setting.

- Their emotional and mental problems may already have been given attention.

The suicide rate is greater for adult pre-trial detainees than for juvenile pre-trial detainees.

Q

QUESTIONS

More suicides are committed by _____ pre-trial detainees than by _____ pre-trial detainees in _____.

(3)

Offenders in state and local prisons and detention facilities have a _____ suicide rate than pre-trial detainees.

(11)

Cautions When Using Suicide Profiles

As you learned earlier, many factors influence the rate of suicides in custody. Using a profile to identify potentially suicidal offenders can be very useful. A profile is a list of traits identified in persons who have committed suicide. In the correctional setting, a profile describes the average offender who commits suicide. It also usually lists several traits that are considered to be major "red flags" for potentially suicidal behavior. These traits include:

- First incarceration
- Accused of heinous crime
- Past or current mental illness
- "Under the influence" upon admission
- History of alcohol/drug abuse

- Significant behavior/mood changes during transport/admission/incarceration
- *Unusual* agitation, particularly in young offenders
- High anxiety—severe or strong physical activity, such as unusual pacing, yelling, swearing, banging
- Prior suicide attempts, including deliberate self-injury gestures (you may see neck and wrist scars)
- Threats of suicide

Many factors influence the rate of suicides in custody.

Q
QUESTIONS

What is a profile?

_____

_____

(8)

Check those behaviors that are "red flags" for potentially suicidal behavior.

_____ A. An offender tells you, "I can't take it anymore. I'd be better off dead."

_____ B. An offender is beginning his third prison term.

_____ C. You observe a newly admitted offender yelling and banging the walls of his cell.

_____ D. You book an offender who is charged with burglary.

(12)

Cautions When Using Suicide Profiles (continued)

A national profile is a good tool. However, a profile developed from offender suicides in your *own system or region* is more reliable.

Whichever profile you use, you must use it carefully. A profile is NOT the most important predictor of suicide. More important predictors are:

- Whether the arresting officer heard or saw anything that may indicate potentially suicidal behavior. For example: "When my employer hears about this in the paper, I know I'll get fired."

- Any significant events that occurred during transportation to the facility. For example: "What will my parents say when they find out what I did?!"

- The arrestee's comments or behavior at admission (intake or booking), or the offender's comments or behavior during incarceration. For example: "I didn't think my life would end like this!"

- Comments from concerned offenders, staff (i.e., clergy), relatives, or significant others. For example: "He talked about suicide. You better watch him closely."

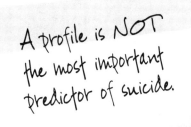

A profile is NOT the most important predictor of suicide.

QUESTIONS

True/False   A profile developed from offender suicides in your own system or region is more reliable than a national profile.

(4)

List four important predictors of suicide.

- _____
- _____
- _____
- _____

(13)

Cautions When Using Suicide Profiles (continued)

You should rank the profile fifth in importance. Tragically, some suicides have occurred because a correctional worker decided that "this offender doesn't fit the profile." In reality, only one trait from the profile may warrant constant or close suicide watch. For example, was the offender under the influence at admission? Does he or she have current or past mental illness? Has he or she made prior suicide attempts or committed a heinous crime?

You should use the suicide profile, therefore, to sensitize yourself to, or increase your awareness of, the signs and symptoms of suicidal behavior—not as the sole factor in determining suicide potential.

QUESTIONS

True/False   When determining an offender's suicide potential, you should rely solely on a profile.

(9)

In reality, only _____ from a suicide profile may warrant constant or close suicide watch.

(14)

This chapter identified the reasons for the difficulty in obtaining reliable statistics on suicides in custody. It discussed the statistical risks for suicides among various types of offenders. It also cited cautions you should exercise when using a suicide profile.

1. List at least two factors that make it difficult to obtain statistics on suicides in custody.

   • Medical examiners or coroners report suicides as "natural deaths" or "unknown causes of death" to save embarrassment to families and/or to protect families from losing insurance payments.

   • Legally, in some states, only a physician or other qualified health personnel can pronounce a person dead; therefore, an offender pronounced dead at a hospital often is not counted as an institutional death.

   • Officials sometimes fail to report suicides.

   • Newspapers sometimes fail to report suicides.

2. Identify the various levels of suicide risk by type of facility.

   • Both juvenile and adult offenders have a higher risk for suicide in short-term facilities (jail/detention) than in long-term facilities (prison/training schools). Moreover, juveniles placed in adult jails commit suicide almost eight times more often than they do in separate juvenile detention facilities.

   • Pre-trial detainees in police lockups and adult detention facilities or jails have the highest rate of suicide.

   • The rate of suicide is greater for adult pre-trial detainees than for juvenile pre-trial detainees in separate juvenile detention facilities.

   • Sentenced/adjudicated offenders in state and local prisons, and training schools/treatment facilities have a lower suicide rate than pre-trial detainees.

3. Define the term "suicide profile" and identify the type that is the most reliable.

   • A profile is a list of traits identified in persons who have committed suicide. In the correctional setting, a profile describes the average offender who commits suicide. It also usually lists several traits that are considered to be major "red flags" for potentially suicidal behavior.

   • The most reliable profile is the one developed from offender suicides in your *own system or region*.

Summary (continued)

4. List at least six traits that are considered to be major "red flags" for potentially suicidal behavior.

   - First incarceration

   - Accused of heinous crime

   - Past or current mental illness

   - "Under the influence" upon admission

   - History of alcohol/drug abuse

   - Significant behavior/mood changes during transport/admission/incarceration

   - *Unusual* agitation, particularly in young offenders

   - High anxiety—severe or strong physical activity, such as unusual pacing, yelling, swearing, banging

   - Prior suicide attempts, including deliberate self-injury gestures (you may see neck and wrist scars)

   - Threats of suicide

5. List four important predictors of potentially suicidal behavior.

   - Whether the arresting officer heard or saw anything that may indicate potentially suicidal behavior

   - Any significant events that occurred during transportation to the facility

   - The arrestee's comments or behavior at admission (intake or booking), or the offender's comments or behavior during incarceration

   - Comments from concerned offenders, staff (i.e., clergy), relatives, or significant others

Answer Key—Research on Suicides in Custody

1. Various factors influence statistics on suicides in custody. They include:

    _____ A. Saving embarrassment to families

    _____ B. Protecting families from losing insurance payments

    _____ C. Allowing only a physician or other qualified health personnel to pronounce a person dead

    __✓__ D. All of the above

2. The highest rate of suicides occurs among:

    _____ A. Parolees

    __✓__ B. Pre-trial detainees

    _____ C. Convicted offenders

    _____ D. Probationers

3. More suicides are committed by **adult** pre-trial detainees than by **juvenile** pre-trial detainees in **separate juvenile detention facilities**.

4. **True**. A profile developed from offender suicides in your own system or region is more reliable than a national profile.

5. **True**. It is difficult to obtain accurate statistics on suicides in custody.

6. Offenders in **short-term** facilities present a higher statistical risk for suicide than offenders in **long-term** facilities.

7. Facilities with the highest suicide rate are:

    _____ A. Lockups

    _____ B. Prisons

    _____ C. Detention facilities

    __✓__ D. Both 1 and 3

8. A profile is a list of traits identified in persons who have committed suicide.

9. **False.** When determining an offender's suicide potential, you first should consider these factors:

    - Whether the arresting officer heard or saw anything that may indicate potentially suicidal behavior

    - Any significant events that occurred during transportation to the facility

    - The arrestee's comments or behavior at admission (intake or booking), or the offender's comments or behavior during incarceration

    - Comments from concerned offenders, staff (i.e., clergy), relatives, or significant others

    Then, you should use the suicide profile.

10. Juveniles in **adult jails** commit suicide almost eight times more often than they do in **separate juvenile detention facilities.**

11. Offenders in state and local prisons and detention facilities have a **lower** suicide rate than pre-trial detainees.

12. Check those behaviors that are "red flags" for potentially suicidal behavior.

    ___✓___ A. An offender tells you, "I can't take it anymore. I'd be better off dead."

    _____ B. An offender is beginning his third prison term.

    ___✓___ C. You observe a newly admitted offender yelling and banging the walls of his cell.

    _____ D. You book an offender who is charged with burglary.

13. Four important predictors of suicide are:

    • Whether the arresting officer heard or saw anything that may indicate potentially suicidal behavior

    • Any significant events that occurred during transportation to the facility

    • The arrestee's comments or behavior at admission (intake or booking), or the offender's comments or behavior during incarceration

    • Comments from concerned offenders, staff (i.e., clergy), relatives, or significant others

14. In reality, only **one trait** from a suicide profile may warrant constant or close suicide watch.

15. **True.** Juveniles must be separated from adults by sight and sound (required by the Juvenile Justice and Delinquency Prevention Act of 1974 for those jurisdictions receiving federal funds under the Act). Unfortunately, this usually means isolating them from staff as well, because staff usually devote their time to the many adult offenders, rather than the one or two juveniles.

16. Over 90 percent of all suicides in custody are committed by **male** offenders.

How Custodial Environments Influence Suicidal Behavior

Objectives

At the end of this chapter, you will be able to:

1. List seven factors of the correctional environment that influence suicidal behavior.

2. Explain how staff's insensitive and negative attitudes influence suicidal behavior.

Introduction

As a correctional worker, you may believe that offenders are well taken care of and have little to complain about. They receive three nutritional meals a day, a clean place to sleep, and adequate clothing. In some cases, offenders are "better off" than they were on the street.

However, incarceration is a traumatic experience for many people. The unique environment in correctional facilities can have a devastating impact on already troubled offenders. Interviews with offenders who attempted suicide verify that it can heavily influence suicidal behavior.

This chapter will identify the environmental factors—psychological, social, and physical—that influence suicidal behavior.

Environmental Factors

Custodial or correctional environments have unique factors that influence suicidal behavior. By becoming aware of and understanding these factors, you can become more effective in identifying and preventing suicides.

Authoritarian Environment: Many persons are not used to a paramilitary setting, where authority and regimentation suddenly become a part of daily life. They are not used to being told what to do, when to do it, and how to do it.

In facilities, rules and regulations guide nearly every action and moment of daily life. Many offenders see the rules as arbitrary and unnecessary. They only seem to be the administration's way of keeping offenders under control.

Most offenders resent the inability to make even the most basic life decisions—when to start the day, what to eat, where to go, and so forth. This approach induces dependence and feelings of childishness as well as insecurity.

No Apparent Control Over the Future: Many offenders, both juveniles and adults, experience feelings of hopelessness and helplessness when placed in confinement. They feel overwhelmed. Their fate is no longer in their control.

QUESTIONS

How do most offenders feel about the inability to make basic decisions about their lives?

_____

_____

(6)

Isolation: For many persons, incarceration is a shocking and traumatic experience. Offenders are deprived of normal access to family and friends—the people who made up their former lives. To many offenders, this experience feels like life is being cut away from them.

The Shame of Incarceration: Many incarcerated persons have strong feelings of shame. Those who feel shame most strongly are often "first-timers" or persons with a limited arrest history.

The Dehumanizing Aspects of Incarceration: Many factors of incarceration are dehumanizing to offenders. Lack of privacy, restricted living space, inability to make their own choices, and association with acting-out individuals especially can have a devastating effect.

Misdemeanants, who commit the most suicides in jails, also develop strong feelings of shame. This group of offenders includes arrestees who have committed minor crimes, such as violating traffic laws or disturbing the peace.

Others who experience deep shame are prominent citizens who commit heinous crimes, or are charged with driving while intoxicated.

Many factors of incarceration are dehumanizing to offenders.

QUESTIONS

Most suicides in jails are committed by:

_____ A. Prominent citizens

_____ B. Misdemeanants

_____ C. Burglars

_____ D. First-timers

(4)

List three factors of incarceration that are dehumanizing to offenders.

• _____

• _____

• _____

(8)

27

Environmental Factors (continued)

Fears: Fear can heighten some offenders' anxieties. Television, movies, and newspapers can instill fear because of the way they portray prison life. Detainees who have spent time in jail or prison may describe true or exaggerated scenarios that make "first timers" highly anxious.

Insensitivity of Workers: Over time, some correctional workers become insensitive to what is happening around them. They lose perspective on how arrest and incarceration can affect the emotions of offenders—especially first-time arrestees.

Some correctional staff cannot control their negative attitudes toward child molesters, same-sex rapists, muggers of elderly women, and/or "white collar" offenders.

Insensitive or negative attitudes and thinking can cloud staff's thinking and cause them to overlook signs and symptoms of potentially suicidal behavior. Staff become victims of their own environment. Any correctional worker can fall victim to this professional tragedy, regardless of his or her title, rank, or level of education.

The best way for staff to learn how to control their insensitive and/or negative attitudes is to participate in self-awareness training and re-training. Staff who *recognize* and *control* their insensitive and/or negative attitudes do a more effective job of suicide prevention than those who don't.

Environmental Factors (continued)

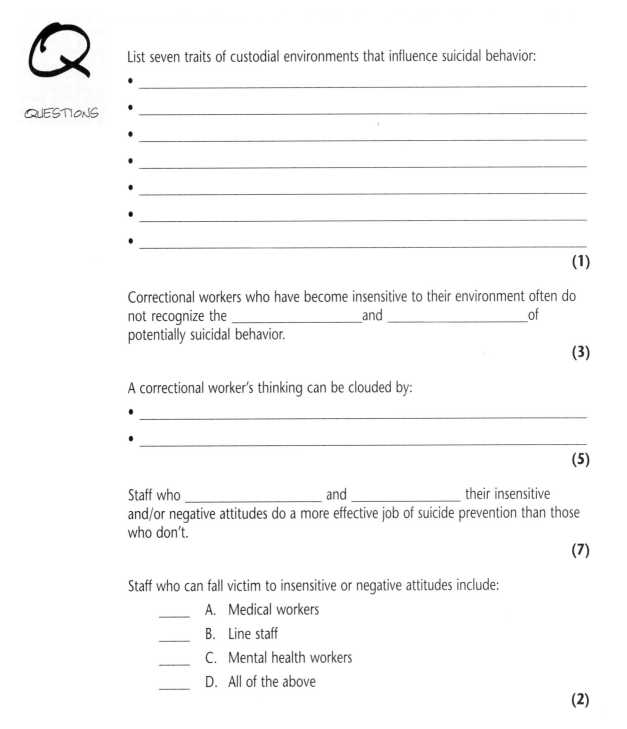

QUESTIONS

List seven traits of custodial environments that influence suicidal behavior:

- _____
- _____
- _____
- _____
- _____
- _____
- _____

(1)

Correctional workers who have become insensitive to their environment often do not recognize the _____ and _____ of potentially suicidal behavior.

(3)

A correctional worker's thinking can be clouded by:

- _____
- _____

(5)

Staff who _____ and _____ their insensitive and/or negative attitudes do a more effective job of suicide prevention than those who don't.

(7)

Staff who can fall victim to insensitive or negative attitudes include:

_____ A. Medical workers

_____ B. Line staff

_____ C. Mental health workers

_____ D. All of the above

(2)

29

CHAPTER 3
How Custodial Environments
Influence Suicidal Behavior

Summary

This chapter identified the environmental factors of correctional facilities—psychological, social, and physical—that influence suicidal behavior.

1. List seven factors of the correctional environment that influence suicidal behavior.

   - The custodial or correctional environment has unique factors that influence suicidal behavior. By becoming aware of and understanding these factors, you can become more effective in identifying and preventing suicides.

     —Authoritarian environment

     —No apparent control over the future

     —Isolation

     —The shame of incarceration

     —The dehumanizing aspects of incarceration

     —Fears

     —Insensitivity of workers

2. Explain how staff's insensitive and negative attitudes influence suicidal behavior.

   - Insensitive or negative attitudes and thinking can cloud staff's thinking and cause them to overlook signs and symptoms of potentially suicidal behavior. Staff become victims of their own environment. Any correctional worker can fall victim to this professional tragedy, regardless of his or her title or rank.

   - The best way for staff to learn how to control their insensitive and/or negative attitudes is to participate in self-awareness training and re-training. Staff who *recognize* and *control* their insensitive and/or negative attitudes do a more effective job of suicide prevention than those who don't.

Answer Key—How Custodial Environments Influence Suicidal Behavior

1. Seven traits of custodial environments that influence suicidal behavior are:
   - Authoritarian environment
   - No apparent control over the future
   - Isolation
   - The shame of incarceration
   - The dehumanizing aspects of incarceration
   - Fears
   - Insensitivity of workers

2. Staff who can fall victim to insensitive or negative attitudes include:
   - _____ A. Medical workers
   - _____ B. Line staff
   - _____ C. Mental health workers
   - __✓__ D. All of the above

3. Correctional workers who have become insensitive to their environment often do not recognize the **signs** and **symptoms** of potentially suicidal behavior.

4. Most suicides in jails are committed by:
   - _____ A. Prominent citizens
   - __✓__ B. Misdemeanants
   - _____ C. Burglars
   - _____ D. First-timers

5. A correctional worker's thinking can be clouded by:
   - Insensitive attitudes
   - Negative attitudes

6. Most offenders become resentful about the inability to make basic life decisions. It induces dependence and feelings of childishness as well as insecurity.

Answer Key— How Custodial Environments Influence Suicidal Behavior (continued)

7. Staff who **recognize** and **control** their insensitive and/or negative attitudes do a more effective job of suicide prevention than those who don't.

8. Factors of incarceration that are dehumanizing to offenders are: (choose three)

   - Lack of privacy

   - Inability to make own choices

   - Association with acting-out individuals

   - Restricted living space

CHAPTER FOUR

Factors Influencing Suicides in Custody

Objectives

At the end of this chapter, you will be able to:

1. Define the term "stress factors" and explain how they influence suicidal behavior.

2. List at least six *internal* stress factors that influence suicidal behavior.

3. List at least six *external* stress factors that influence suicidal behavior.

Introduction

We have discussed how the correctional environment can influence suicidal behavior. At this point, you may be thinking, "The environment can't be the only factor that plays a role in offender suicides." If so, you are correct.

There are a number of *stress factors* that influence suicide. For many offenders, the presence of one or more of these factors may be the "last straw" leading to suicide. Identifying these factors in offenders, therefore, is the first step in suicide prevention.

This chapter will discuss what stress factors are and how they influence suicidal behavior. Then it will identify both internal and external stress factors that can lead to suicide.

Stress Factors

Each of us has a "breaking point." Many people are able to "weather the storm," pick themselves up, and go on with their lives. Some people, however, react differently. For them, the storm proves too much, and they attempt suicide.

What causes a person to reach a "breaking point"? The answer can be found in stress factors. They put a person in a certain frame of mind and, thus, cause him or her to act in a certain way. These factors greatly influence suicide; they are either personal or situational.

Q

QUESTIONS

True/False   Suicide potential is a fixed, unchanging condition.

(2)

True/False   Only emotionally unstable persons have "breaking points."

(8)

What are stress factors?

_____

_____

_____

_____

(6)

Internal Stress Factors

Internal stress factors are the personal forces that make a person more vulnerable to suicidal behavior. They include:

✔ Previously been imprisoned and not wanting to face new charges.

✔ Possibly involved in same-sex rape or other offender victimization.

✔ Impulsivity (which influences suicide and is greater in a young person).

✔ Prior suicide attempt or suicidal thoughts.

✔ Recent suicide attempt or suicidal thoughts.

✔ History of alcohol/drug abuse; a long history is more significant.

✔ History of mental illness, with having been hospitalized considered the most significant factor.

✔ Prior alcohol or drug withdrawal experience (and not wanting to undergo the painful physical and psychological ordeal again).

✔ Severe guilt or shame over crime; may be more than the seriousness of the offense. Most offenders who commit suicide have been charged with or convicted of *minor* offenses.

✔ Current mental illness, including clinical depression and *situational* depression, which passes when the temporary crisis is resolved. We will discuss depression in Chapter 5.

✔ Terminal illness or chronic medical condition, e.g., AIDS or chemical dependency.

Q

QUESTIONS

Five internal stress factors that influence suicidal behavior are:

• _____

• _____

• _____

• _____

• _____

(4)

External Stress Factors

External stress factors are the situational or conditional forces that push a person toward suicidal behavior. They include:

✔ First-time arrest, or insignificant arrest history. Two national jail studies revealed that 35 percent of suicide deaths were committed by first-time arrestees or those with insignificant arrest histories.

✔ Being under the influence of alcohol/drugs upon admission. Over 60 percent of all jail suicides are committed by offenders who were under the influence of alcohol/drugs upon admission.

✔ Loss of stabilizing resources such as:

— Loved one (for a juvenile it may be a peer rather than a family member)

— Recent job loss or failure to perform well

— Expulsion from school

— Loss of home, farm, or other business

— Financial loss

✔ Rejection by loved ones or peers, or perceptions of such. For example, an offender receives a "Dear John" letter that says, "I am divorcing you. I can't wait eight years for you to get out of prison."

✔ Manipulation for secondary gains—e.g., different housing, another facility (like mental health), or dismissed charge(s)—that is not recognized by staff and/or not professionally handled. For example, an offender is unhappy with his living situation (custodial environment). He has studied the officer's pattern of making rounds and plans to attempt suicide, "knowing" that he will be rescued. Unfortunately, an emergency occurs and the officer must delay his regular round. The offender's manipulation ends in death. Properly trained officers usually can prevent such tragic scenarios by knowing the inmates (under their supervision), observing behavior/mood changes, and fostering a climate in which this type of manipulation will not happen.

✔ Incarceration for heinous crime.

✔ Victim of same-sex rape or threat of it.

✔ Citizens who are prominent in the community. "The higher in society, the greater the fall," must be recognized.

✔ Harsh, condemning, rejecting attitudes of correctional workers, including mental health counselors.

✔ History of suicide in the family.

✔ Long sentences in correctional institutions that have adverse conditions and a poor quality of life.

✔ Recent suicide or attempt in facility, which may trigger "copycat" attempts.

Many suicides would never have occurred without stress factors. Unfortunately, the presence of one or more of these factors can push an individual to the "breaking point." Unable to handle the situation or "weather the storm," the person commits suicide.

Good suicide prevention in custody, therefore, demands properly trained, positive-minded correctional workers who can identify stress factors. Indeed, identifying these factors is the first step in preventing suicides.

Q

QUESTIONS

Five external stress factors that influence suicidal behavior are:

• _____

• _____

• _____

• _____

• _____

(3)

Personal forces are _____,
situational or conditional forces are _____.

(5)

Over _____ percent of persons who commit suicide in jails are under the influence of alcohol/drugs upon admission.

(7)

The attitudes of direct service workers may either _____ or _____ to suicides.

(1)

The first step in suicide prevention is:

_____ A. Hospitalizing the offender

_____ B. Identifying internal and external stress factors

_____ C. Referring the offender to mental health staff

_____ D. Ignoring the offender's manipulative behavior

(9)

Summary

This chapter discussed what stress factors are and how they influence suicidal behavior. It also identified the internal and external stressors that can lead to suicide.

1. Define the term "stress factors" and explain how they influence suicidal behavior.

   - Stress factors put a person in a certain frame of mind and, thus, cause him or her to act in a certain way. They can push an individual to the "breaking point." Unable to handle the situation or "weather the storm," the person commits suicide.

2. List at least six *internal* stress factors that influence suicidal behavior.

   - *Internal* stress factors are the personal forces that make a person more vulnerable to suicidal behavior.

     — Previously been imprisoned and not wanting to face new charges

     — Possibly involved in same-sex rape or other offender victimization

     — Impulsivity (which is greater in a young person)

     — Prior suicide attempt or suicidal thoughts

     — Recent suicide attempt or suicidal thoughts

     — History of alcohol/drug abuse; a long history is more significant

     — History of mental illness, with having been hospitalized considered the most significant factor

     — Prior alcohol or drug withdrawal experience (and not wanting to undergo the painful physical and psychological ordeal again)

     — Severe guilt or shame over crime

     — Current mental illness, including clinical depression and *situational* depression

     — Terminal illness or chronic medical condition

3. List at least six *external* stress factors that influence suicidal behavior.

   - *External* stress factors are the situational or conditional forces that push a person toward suicidal behavior.

     — First-time arrest, or insignificant arrest history

     — Being under the influence of alcohol/drugs upon admission

     — Loss of stabilizing resources

     — Rejection by loved ones or peers, or perceptions of such

     — Manipulation for secondary gains that is not recognized by staff and/or not professionally handled

     — Incarceration for heinous crime

     — Victim of same-sex rape or threat of it

     — Citizens who are prominent in the community

     — Harsh, condemning, rejecting attitudes of correctional workers, including mental health counselors

     — History of suicide in the family

     — Long sentences in correctional institutions that have adverse conditions and a poor quality of life

     — Recent suicide or attempt in facility, which may trigger "copycat" attempts

   - Identifying internal and external stress factors is the first step in preventing suicides.

Answer Key—Factors Influencing Suicides in Custody

1. The attitudes of direct service workers may either **prevent** or **lead** to suicides.

2. **False.** Suicide potential is **not** a fixed, unchanging condition.

3. External stress factors that influence suicidal behavior are: (choose five)

   - First-time arrest or insignificant arrest history
   - Being under the influence of alcohol/drugs upon admission
   - Loss of stabilizing resources
   - Rejection by loved ones or peers, or perceptions of such
   - Manipulation for secondary gains that is not recognized by staff and/or not professionally handled
   - Incarceration for heinous crime
   - Victim of same-sex rape or threat of it
   - Citizens who are prominent in the community
   - Harsh, condemning, rejecting attitudes of correctional workers, including mental health counselors
   - History of suicide in the family
   - Long sentences in correctional institutions that have adverse conditions and a poor quality of life
   - Recent suicide or attempt in facility, which may trigger "copycat" attempts

4. Internal stress factors that influence suicidal behavior are: (choose five)

   - Previously been imprisoned and not wanting to face new charges
   - Possibly involved in same-sex rape or other offender victimization
   - Impulsivity (which is greater in a young person)
   - Prior suicide attempt or suicidal thoughts
   - Recent suicide attempt or suicidal thoughts
   - History of alcohol/drug abuse; a long history is more significant
   - History of mental illness, with having been hospitalized considered the most significant factor
   - Prior alcohol or drug withdrawal experience (and not wanting to undergo the painful physical and psychological ordeal again)
   - Severe guilt or shame over crime
   - Current mental illness, including clinical depression and *situational* depression
   - Terminal illness or chronic medical condition

4

Answer Key—Factors Influencing Suicides in Custody (continued)

5. Personal forces are **internal stress factors**; situational or conditional forces are **external stress factors**.

6. Stress factors put a person in a certain frame of mind and, thus, cause him or her to act in a certain way. These factors greatly influence suicide; they are either internal or external.

7. Over **60** percent of persons who commit suicide in jails are under the influence of alcohol/drugs upon admission.

8. **False.** Each of us has a "breaking point."

9. The first step in suicide prevention is:

    _____ A. Hospitalizing the offender

    ✓ B. Identifying internal and external stress factors

    _____ C. Referring the offender to mental health staff

    _____ D. Ignoring the offender's manipulative behavior

Signs and Symptoms of Suicidal Behavior

Objectives

At the end of this chapter, you will be able to:

1. List at least 12 signs and symptoms of potentially suicidal behavior in offenders.

2. List at least ten signs/symptoms of depression.

3. Describe the "improving and must be okay" fallacy related to depression.

4. Identify why it is important to distinguish between usual and unusual agitation.

5. List at least three signs/symptoms of unusual agitation.

Introduction

We have discussed how internal and external stress factors can push a person to the "breaking point." Unable to cope, the person attempts suicide. Knowing an offender has one or more of these factors can alert you to a possible suicide risk.

Another way to identify a potentially suicidal offender is to know the signs and symptoms exhibited by a person who is "being pushed" or has reached the "breaking point." When they are suicidal, most offenders exhibit these red flags. Rarely does a suicide occur without the appearance of several signs and symptoms. Often, however, only one or two signs and symptoms can alert a trained, positive-minded correctional worker to a potentially suicidal offender.

This chapter will identify the signs and symptoms of potentially suicidal behavior. The chapter will discuss depression and agitation in detail because they are critical warning signs of suicide.

45

Warning Signs and Symptoms of Suicidal Behavior

Suicidal offenders exhibit a variety of traits and behaviors, or signs and symptoms. The key signs and symptoms are:

- Current depression (depression is the best sign of suicide).

- Strong guilt or shame over the offense, which often is a misdemeanor.

- Threats of suicide; makes statements that are death-related or imply finality, e.g., "I can't take it anymore; I've had it."

- Prior suicide attempts, including deliberate self-harm gestures such as cutting one's wrist or neck.

- Current or prior mental illness, particularly paranoid delusions (having an *irrational* thought that others are out to harm them)

or hallucinations (believing that they hear, taste, feel, or smell something that is not there). Command hallucinations are usually associated with suicide. A person suffering from this type of hallucination hears voices that tell him to kill himself.

- Unusual agitation or aggression, particularly by a juvenile.

- Being under the influence of alcohol/drugs at arrest. Depression sets in when the person sobers up, leading to a suicide attempt. Also, fear of going through withdrawal triggers some suicide attempts.

- History of alcohol/drug abuse.

- Projection of hopelessness or helplessness—no sense of the future.

Warning Signs and Symptoms of Suicidal Behavior (continued)

KEY signs & symptoms of suicidal behavior are:

- Depression
- Strong guilt / shame
- History of mental illness
- Previous suicide attempts / threats
- Behavior / mood changes
- Drug and alcohol abuse

QUESTIONS

True/False   Suicides rarely occur without some signs and symptoms being displayed.

(2)

True/False   The best indicator of suicide is guilt.

(8)

Warning Signs and Symptoms of Suicidal Behavior (continued)

Additional signs and symptoms of depression include but are not limited to:

- Unusual concern over what will happen in the legal process—e.g., finding of guilt, and sentencing.

- Noticeable mood and/or behavior changes.

- Period of calm following agitation; the person regains his energy and may decide to kill himself.

- Increasing difficulty in relating to others.

- Unrealistic talk about getting out of the facility.

- Inability to deal effectively with the present—preoccupied with the past.

- Packing belongings.

- Giving away possessions.

- Attention-getting gestures by self-harm. *Caution*: Some offenders who manipulate for secondary gain(s) do kill themselves; each gesture must be managed as the *first* real suicide attempt.

- Excessive risk-taking, particularly among young offenders.

Only the positive minded, "we-type" team worker will likely notice many of the suicide signs and symptoms listed above. The "I-me" worker probably will not observe them.

"We-type" correctional workers are the ones who follow established policies, procedures, and job descriptions. They also reasonably control their negative attitudes. "I-me" workers, however, do not adhere to such practices. They are usually self-centered, arrogant, and frequently unable to control their negative attitudes. These workers also tend to abuse power and authority.

Q

List three key signs and symptoms of suicide.

• _____

• _____

• _____

(4)

True/False   Manipulators rarely attempt suicide.

(9)

Write a "T" next to the statement if it is a sign or symptom that might be displayed by suicidal persons; write an "F" if it is not.

_____   1. Get along well with others

_____   2. Do not take risks

_____   3. Give away possessions

_____   4. Are preoccupied with the present

_____   5. Go through a period of calm following agitation

_____   6. Talk about getting out of the facility, when in reality they cannot

_____   7. Injure themselves to get attention

_____   8. Are unusually agitated

_____   9. Feel hopeless or helpless

_____   10. Threaten to commit suicide

_____   11. Hear voices that tell them to kill themselves

_____   12. Have an unusual concern over what will happen

_____   13. Unpack belongings and carefully put away items

_____   14. Are sober at arrest

(6)

Depression

Many people often confuse "the blues" with serious depression. A person who feels sad or "down" when things are not going well has the blues. Nearly everyone has this feeling from time to time. A person who constantly feels sad and "down," though, may be experiencing depression.

Depressed people see no meaning in life and cannot seem to enjoy anything. They are prone to suicide.

Indeed, depression is the best sign of suicide risk. Approximately 70 to 80 percent of all suicidal individuals show signs of depression.

Common signs and symptoms of depression are:

Mood

- Extreme sadness or doom-and-gloom perspective, e.g., "Life isn't worth it—things would be better with me gone"
- Excessive crying
- Loss of interest in activities, people, and appearance
- Significant and sudden mood variations

Thought

- Pessimism concerning future
- Strong guilt feeling
- Low self-esteem—"I'm no good!"
- Feeling of inability to go on
- Excessive self-blaming, even about a misdemeanor
- Difficulty in thinking, concentrating

Behavior and Appearance

- Withdrawal or silence
- Loss or increase of appetite and/or weight
- Sleeping problems—too much or too little
- High anxiety or tension
- Downcast eyes/looks
- Lethargy (sluggishness, a stupor-like state)
- Writing or leaving suicide notes
- Talk of suicide, even when what is said appears to be in jest
- Neglect of personal appearance

Suicidal offenders commonly have situational or reactive depression related to a negative event. For example, their child is seriously hurt, or their spouse loses his or her job. When the situation is resolved, the depression disappears. Clinical, long-term depression usually occurs in only a small percentage of suicidal offenders.

Note: Depressed persons often commit suicide when their symptoms appear to be improving. This happens because depression often robs the individual of the energy and resolution to act forcefully. As the depressed person begins to improve, the ability to act returns. He now has the will and energy to carry out the suicide act. Correctional workers at *all* levels have been "caught off guard" with this phenomenon, resulting in completed suicides.

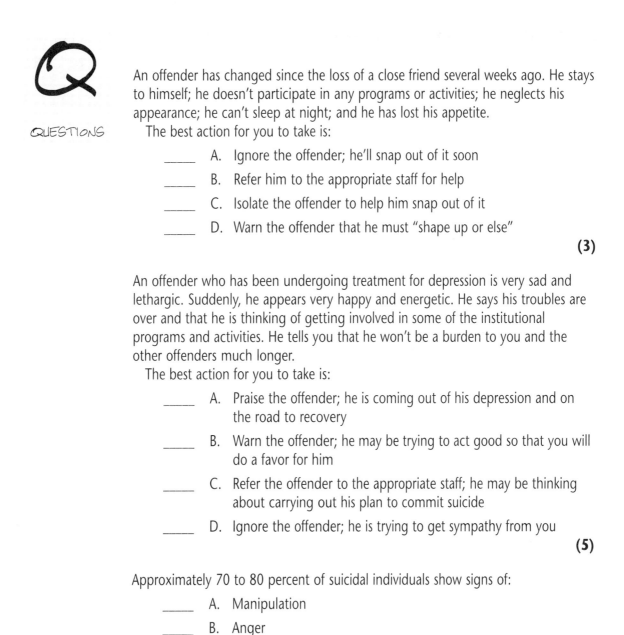

QUESTIONS

An offender has changed since the loss of a close friend several weeks ago. He stays to himself; he doesn't participate in any programs or activities; he neglects his appearance; he can't sleep at night; and he has lost his appetite.

The best action for you to take is:

_____ A. Ignore the offender; he'll snap out of it soon

_____ B. Refer him to the appropriate staff for help

_____ C. Isolate the offender to help him snap out of it

_____ D. Warn the offender that he must "shape up or else"

(3)

An offender who has been undergoing treatment for depression is very sad and lethargic. Suddenly, he appears very happy and energetic. He says his troubles are over and that he is thinking of getting involved in some of the institutional programs and activities. He tells you that he won't be a burden to you and the other offenders much longer.

The best action for you to take is:

_____ A. Praise the offender; he is coming out of his depression and on the road to recovery

_____ B. Warn the offender; he may be trying to act good so that you will do a favor for him

_____ C. Refer the offender to the appropriate staff; he may be thinking about carrying out his plan to commit suicide

_____ D. Ignore the offender; he is trying to get sympathy from you

(5)

Approximately 70 to 80 percent of suicidal individuals show signs of:

_____ A. Manipulation

_____ B. Anger

_____ C. Depression

_____ D. Schizophrenia

(7)

Agitation

Most correctional workers agree that agitation usually exists in correctional facilities. Offenders often are tense, anxious, and emotional—for example, angry or irritated. The problem arises when you ask correctional workers to distinguish between *usual* and *unusual* agitation. Many correctional workers cannot do so.

Distinguishing between usual and unusual agitation is an important part of suicide prevention. *Unusual* agitation, followed by a period of calm, often precedes suicide. During this calm period, the offender regains his energy and may decide to kill himself. Another strong sign of potentially suicidal behavior is *unusual agitation, combined with aggression*—especially by young offenders.

The positive-minded, properly trained correctional worker usually notices these "red flag" behaviors and prevents the suicides.

Signs and symptoms of unusual agitation are:

- A high level of tension
- Extreme anxiety
  - —Severe or strong physical activity, such as unusual pacing, yelling, swearing, banging
- Strong emotions
  - —Guilt
  - —Rage
  - —Wish for revenge

QUESTIONS

For the past three days, an offender has been very tense and experiencing rage attacks. Today, you notice that he is calm and quiet. Should you be concerned about the offender's behavior. If so, why?

_____

_____

_____

_____

(1)

This chapter identified the signs and symptoms of potentially suicidal behavior. The chapter discussed depression and agitation in detail because they are critical signs of suicide.

1. List at least 12 signs and symptoms of potentially suicidal behavior in offenders.

   • Rarely does a suicide occur without the appearance of several signs and symptoms. Often, however, only one or two signs and symptoms can alert a trained, positive-minded correctional worker to a potentially suicidal offender.

   • Key signs and symptoms are:

     — Current depression

     — Strong guilt or shame over the offense, which often is a misdemeanor

     — Threats of suicide; makes statements that are death-related or imply finality

     — Prior suicide attempts, including deliberate self-harm gestures

     — Current or prior mental illness, particularly paranoid delusions or hallucinations

     — Unusual agitation or aggression, particularly by a juvenile

     — Being under the influence of alcohol/drugs at arrest

     — History of alcohol/drug abuse

     — Projection of hopelessness or helplessness—no sense of the future

     — Unusual concern over what will happen during the legal process

     — Noticeable mood and/or behavior changes

     — Period of calm following agitation

     — Increasing difficulty in relating to others

     — Unrealistic talk about getting out of the facility

     — Inability to deal effectively with the present—preoccupied with the past

     — Packing belongings

     — Giving away possessions

     — Attention-getting gestures by self-harm (*Caution*: Some offenders who manipulate for secondary gain(s) do kill themselves; each gesture must be managed as the *first* real suicide attempt.)

     — Excessive risk-taking, particularly among young offenders

   • Only the positive minded, "we-type" team worker will likely notice many of the suicide signs and symptoms listed above. The "I-me" worker probably will not observe them.

2. List at least ten signs/symptoms of depression.

   • Persons who usually feel sad and "down" may be experiencing depression.

   • Depression is the best sign of suicide. Approximately 70 to 80 percent of suicidal individuals show signs of depression.

CHAPTER 5
Signs and Symptoms of
Suicidal Behavior

Summary (continued)

Mood

- Extreme sadness or doom-and-gloom perspective
- Excessive crying
- Loss of interest in activities, people, and appearance
- Significant and sudden mood variations

Thought

- Pessimism concerning future
- Strong guilt feeling
- Low self-esteem
- Feeling of inability to go on
- Excessive self-blaming, even about a misdemeanor
- Difficulty in thinking, concentrating

Behavior and Appearance

- Withdrawal or silence
- Loss or increase of appetite and/or weight
- Sleeping problems—too much or too little
- High anxiety or tension
- Downcast eyes/looks
- Lethargy (sluggishness, a stupor-like state)
- Writing or leaving suicide notes

- Talk of suicide, even when what is said appears to be in jest
- Neglect of personal appearance

3. Describe the "improving and must be okay" fallacy related to depression.

- Depressed persons often attempt suicide when their symptoms appear to be improving. This happens because depression often robs the individual of the energy and resolution to act forcefully. As the depressed person begins to improve, the ability to act returns. He now has the will and energy to carry out the suicide act.

4. Identify why it is important to distinguish between usual and unusual agitation.

- Distinguishing between usual and unusual agitation is an important part of suicide prevention. *Unusual* agitation, followed by a period of calm, often precedes suicide. Another strong sign of potentially suicidal behavior is unusual agitation, combined with aggression— especially by young offenders.

5. List at least three signs/symptoms of unusual agitation.

- A high level of tension
- Extreme anxiety
- Strong emotions

Answer Key—Signs and Symptoms of Suicidal Behavior

1. Yes, you should be concerned about the offender's behavior because he was **unusually** agitated (very tense and showing strong emotions—rage attacks) and then suddenly became calm. **Unusual agitation, followed by a period of calm, often precedes suicide.**

2. **True.** Suicides rarely occur without some signs and symptoms being displayed.

3. The best action to take is:

   _____ A. Ignore the offender: he'll snap out of it soon

   __✓__ B. Refer him to the appropriate staff for help

   _____ C. Isolate the offender to help him snap out of it

   _____ D. Warn the offender that he must "shape up or else"

   The symptoms—disturbed sleep, loss of appetite, loss of interest in activities, and neglect of appearance—all suggest depression, one of the signs of potentially suicidal behavior.

4. Key signs and symptoms of potentially suicidal behavior include: (choose three)

   - Depression
   - History of mental illness
   - Previous suicide attempts/threats
   - Drug and alcohol abuse
   - Behavior/mood changes
   - Strong guilt/shame

5. The best action to take is:

   _____ A. Praise the offender; he is coming out of his depression and on the road to recovery

   _____ B. Warn the offender; he may be trying to act good so that you will do a favor for him

   __✓__ C. Refer the offender to the appropriate staff; he may be thinking about carrying out his plan to commit suicide

   _____ D. Ignore the offender; he is trying to get sympathy from you

   Depression can be most dangerous when it seems to be improving. The depressed offender usually doesn't have the energy or initiative to attempt suicide. But when he comes out of the depression, he has the necessary energy and resolve to put the suicidal plan into action.

Answer Key—Signs and Symptoms of Suicidal Behavior (continued)

6. Write a "T" next to the statement if it is a sign or symptom that might be displayed by suicidal persons; write an "F" if it is not.

      F   1. Get along well with others [increasing difficulty in relating to others]

      F   2. Do not take risks [engage in excessive risk-taking]

      T   3. Give away possessions

      F   4. Are preoccupied with the present [are preoccupied with the past]

      T   5. Go through a period of calm following agitation

      T   6. Talk about getting out of the facility, when in reality they cannot

      T   7. Injure themselves to get attention

      T   8. Are unusually agitated

      T   9. Feel hopeless or helpless

      T   10. Threaten to commit suicide

      T   11. Hear voices that tell them to kill themselves

      T   12. Have an unusual concern over what will happen

      F   13. Unpack belongings and carefully put them away [pack belongings]

      F   14. Are sober at arrest [under the influence of alcohol/drugs at arrest]

7. Approximately 70 to 80 percent of suicidal individuals show signs of:

      _____   A. Manipulation

      _____   B. Anger

       ✓   C. Depression

      _____   D. Schizophrenia

8. **False.** The best indicator of suicide is **depression**.

9. **False.** Research shows that at least one-third of suicide deaths appear to be associated with manipulative efforts.

CHAPTER SIX

Assessing Suicide Risk: The Initial Health Screening and Clearance

Objectives

At the end of this chapter, you will be able to:

1. Identify the four parts of a health screening.

2. Identify six conditions for which medical and mental health clearance should be required before admitting an arrestee into custody.

3. List at least four observational questions related to identifying suicidal behavior.

4. List at least four interview questions related to identifying suicidal behavior.

5. List at least four guidelines for conducting a successful health screening interview.

6. Identify six guidelines for making an appropriate disposition or referral.

Introduction

The first crucial high-risk period for suicide is during the first 24 hours of incarceration. In pre-trial/pre-adjudication detention facilities, nearly one-third of suicide deaths occur within three hours after admission. Therefore, identifying potentially suicidal offenders *before* they are incarcerated is critical. Properly trained admissions workers can detect potentially suicidal offenders about 90 percent of the time during the initial health screening.

This chapter will review the initial health screening and clearance processes. It will examine how to conduct a proper health screening of a newly admitted offender. In particular, it will focus on how to conduct an effective interview with the offender. It also will discuss the medical and mental health clearances.

Health Assessment

All national standards require offenders to be assessed for medical and mental health fitness *upon arrival* at the facility.

Some institutions, especially large ones, assign nurses or emergency medical technicians to do health screenings. At most facilities, however, trained/experienced correctional workers are responsible for screening offenders prior to admission. In either approach, admissions staff often make referrals to in-house or community mental health workers who, in turn, make the final decision about suicide risk and offender management. (Statutes and agency practices usually specify who will make the final decision on suicide risk—a psychiatrist, psychologist, social worker, psychiatric nurse, and so forth.)

QUESTIONS

The first crucial high-risk period for suicide is during the first _____ of incarceration.

(6)

All national standards require that facilities determine the medical and mental health fitness of _____ offenders upon arrival at the facility.

(14)

Correctional workers can effectively do a *preliminary screening* or assessment of the offender's health. This assessment includes identifying the signs and symptoms of suicide. However, the medical and mental health *clearances* must be done by qualified professionals.

Health Screening

Unlike the medical and mental health clearances, the health screening is usually done by an admissions worker and consists of four parts:

- Asking the arresting or transportation officer questions

- Observing the new offender

- Asking the offender questions

Correctional workers can effectively do a preliminary screening or assessment of the offender's health.

- Making a disposition/referral, based on the information gathered during the screening process

Some facilities ask the offender to fill out the Health Screening Form. Experts do not recommend this procedure because the individual may have only a limited understanding of the questions being asked.

Take a few moments now and review the entire sample form to get an idea of what the health screening process is all about. Then, proceed to the first part of the process: Asking the arresting or transportation officer questions.

Sample Health Screening Form

Sample Health Screening Form for Subjects Held in Custody

Date _____

Subject's† Name/Number _____

Admission Worker's Name _____

Arresting/Transportation Officer Questions

	Yes*	No
1. Did you detect any signs/symptoms of suicidal behavior?	_____	_____
2. Did you notice any other health problems?	_____	_____

Admissions Worker's Observations

	Yes	No
3. Does the subject have any injury, or is he or she in any pain?	_____	_____
4. Does the subject have any signs of infection?	_____	_____
5. Does the subject appear to be under the influence of alcohol and/or drugs?	_____	_____
6. Does the subject have any signs of alcohol and/or drug withdrawal?	_____	_____
7. Does the subject appear to be suicidal?	_____	_____
Does the subject have wrist/neck scars?	_____	_____
8. Does the subject appear to be mentally ill?	_____	_____
9. Does the subject's behavior suggest risk of assault?	_____	_____
10. Does the subject appear to be mentally retarded?	_____	_____
11. Is the subject small, frail, seemingly weak?	_____	_____
12. Does the subject appear to be effeminate?	_____	_____
13. Does the subject appear to be naive, unsophisticated?	_____	_____
14. Is the subject carrying medication?	_____	_____

Admissions Worker/Subject Questions

Note: Before asking any questions, please say: "I am going to ask you some questions now. We ask these same questions of everybody who comes here because we're interested in their health and welfare."

	Yes	No	Refused to Answer
15. Are you presently taking any medication?	_____	_____	_____
If *yes*, for what? _____			
What type of medication? _____			
16. Do you use alcohol?	_____	_____	_____
If *yes*, how often? _____			
How much do you drink? _____			
When were you drunk last? _____			
When did you last take a drink? _____			
17. Do you use any street drugs?	_____	_____	_____

†The term "subject" is used on this form instead of arrestee, inmate, or juvenile.
*For each "Yes" response, you should provide specific information under the "Remarks" section at the end of the form.

Sample Health Screening Form (continued)

	Yes	No	Refused to Answer
If *yes*, what type(s)? _____			
How often do you take drugs? _____			
When did you last take drugs? _____			
When were you high last? _____			
18. Is this the first time you have ever been confined?	_____	_____	_____
19. Have you ever thought about or attempted to commit suicide?	_____	_____	_____
Are you *now* concerned that you might attempt to commit suicide?	_____		
20. Do you have any medical or mental problems now?	_____	_____	_____
If *yes*, are you receiving any treatment for the problems?	_____	_____	_____
If *yes*, what is the treatment? _____			
21. Have you had any previous mental or emotional problems?	_____	_____	_____
If *yes*, were you ever hospitalized for those problems?	_____	_____	_____
22. If the subject is *female*, ask:			
Are you pregnant?	_____	_____	_____
If *yes*, how many months? _____			
23. Are you on any special diet?	_____	_____	_____
If *yes*, what kind of diet is it and why are you on it? _____			
24. Is there anything special that we should know about you for your welfare or protection?	_____	_____	_____
If *yes*, what? _____			

DISPOSITION OR REFERRAL TO: (Please check applicable response):*

_____ Emergency care (state where): _____

_____ General population

_____ Close supervision, e.g., potential same-sex rape victim

_____ Sick call

_____ Placed in two-person cell or room (_____) (for communicable disease cases)

_____ Placed in suicide-resistant observation cell/room under constant supervision (high-risk suicide case)

_____ Placed in two- or more person cell/room or dormitory (_____) under special/close observation (suicidal offender)

NOTE: All these responses require documented action (i.e., state the basis for your disposition in the Remarks section). Follow your facility's "Guidelines for Disposition."

REMARKS: _____

_____

_____

The American Medical Association Jail Project originally developed this form. American Health Care Consultants and the National Commission on Correctional Health Care, both of Chicago, later revised it. Juvenile and Criminal Justice International of Roseville, Minnesota, modified the form further to better suit it to individual facilities.

*Your facility should have its own disposition checklist that reflects its resources and procedures. This checklist merely shows a sample approach that follows recognized practices.

Health Screening

Q

QUESTIONS

List the four parts of the Health Screening Form.

- _____
- _____
- _____
- _____

(11)

After you mark "Yes" to a question on the Health Screening Form, you should:

_____ A. Write notes in the margin next to the question

_____ B. Proceed directly to the next question

_____ C. Write down the specifics in the "Remarks" section

_____ D. Tell the offender about it

(17)

Sample List of Symptoms of Medical/Psychological Illnesses

When you're completing the Health Screening Form, you probably will need to have available a list of the symptoms of different medical and psychological illnesses to use as a reference guide. Your facility most likely will provide you with one that looks similar to the list below.

Injury

- Profuse bleeding
- Profuse sweating
- Vomiting
- Difficulty breathing
- Severe headache, had sudden onset

Infection

- Yellow skin
- Poor skin condition
    —Rash
    —Sores
    —Spots
    —Scabs
- Weakness
- Respiratory distress

- Diarrhea
- Cramps
- Swollen lymph nodes
- Chronic cough/phlegm
- Uncontrolled vomiting

Under the Influence of Alcohol/Drugs

- Slurred speech
- "Bloodshot"/red eyes
- Dilated pupils (expanded, large)
- Unsteady walk
- Confused/disoriented
- Vomiting
- Sleepy or hyperactive

Alcohol and/or Drug Withdrawal

- Sweating
- Shaking severely
- Nauseous/vomiting
- Delirious
- Hallucinating
- Difficulty breathing
- Pinpoint pupils (tiny, extremely small)

Health Screening (continued)

Suicidal Signs and Symptoms

- Guilt or shame over the offense
- Current or prior mental illness, particularly paranoid delusions or hallucinations
- Depression
  - —Sadness
  - —Crying
  - —Mood variations
  - —Pessimism about future
  - —Low self-esteem
  - —Feelings of inability to go on
  - —Guilt or shame over the offense
  - —Difficulty in thinking, concentrating
  - —Withdrawal/silence
  - —Anxiety or tension
  - —Downcast eyes/looks
  - —Lethargy (sluggishness, a stupor-like state)

- Talk of suicide
- Prior suicide attempts
- Unusual agitation or aggression, particularly in a juvenile
  - —Period of calm following agitation
  - —High level of tension
  - —Extreme anxiety
  - —Strong emotions
    - Guilt
    - Rage
    - Wish for revenge
- Projection of hopelessness or helplessness—no sense of future
- Unusual concern over what will happen
- Inability to deal effectively with the present—preoccupied with the past
- Noticeable behavior changes
- Under the influence of drugs/alcohol
- History of alcohol/drug abuse

Mental Illness

- Hearing voices
- Withdrawn/uncommunicative
- Hallucinating
- Behaving erratically

Mental Retardation

- Difficulty understanding questions/comments
- *Slowness* in reacting/understanding
- Short attention span
- Weak/shortened memory
- Language problems

QUESTIONS

Match the common symptoms with their corresponding medical/psychological illnesses.

1. Injury
2. Infection
3. Under the influence of alcohol/drugs
4. Alcohol and/or drug withdrawal
5. Suicide signs and symptoms
6. Mental illness
7. Mental retardation

_____ A. Slowness in reacting/understanding

_____ B. Depression

_____ C. Slurred speech

_____ D. Hearing voices

_____ E. Language problems

_____ F. Significant bleeding

_____ G. Yellow skin

_____ H. Severe shaking

_____ I. Erratic behavior

_____ J. Chronic cough/phlegm

(20)

Step 1: Asking the Arresting or Transportation Officer Questions

The first step of the screening process is asking the arresting or transportation officer questions. This officer may have valuable information that can help you prevent a suicide.

Three reasons arresting or transportation officers might have such information are:

- Levels of anxiety often are higher at arrest. Thus, the arrestee may talk to the transportation officer to relieve anxiety. Indeed, under these circumstances, the arrestee may talk more readily and make frank comments— perhaps about suicide.

- Sentenced offenders may be concerned about confinement in a facility; they may have a "fear of the unknown." Thus, sentenced offenders may talk to transportation officers to relieve anxiety.

- Offenders often perceive transportation officers as neutral persons and talk freely with them. Transportation officers who have had training to be good listeners usually can pick up valuable information.

QUESTIONS

Why might offenders talk to arresting or transportation officers?

_____

_____

_____

_____

(4)

Asking the Arresting or Transportation Officer Questions (continued)

Basically, you should ask the arresting/transportation officer the following two questions that appear on the Health Screening Form. These questions focus on the arresting/transportation officer's observations of the offender.

Sample Health Screening Form for Subjects Held in Custody

Date _____

Subject's Name/Number _____

Admission Worker's Name _____

Arresting/Transportation Officer Questions	Yes	No
1. Did you detect any signs/symptoms of suicidal behavior?	_____	_____
2. Did you notice any other health problems?	_____	_____

Be sure to follow up any "Yes" responses by writing specific information in the "Remarks" section at the end of the form.

QUESTIONS

True/False You should ask the arresting/transportation officer directly whether the offender appeared to be suicidal or appeared to have other health problems.

(15)

Step 2: Observing the New Offender

The second step of the screening process is observing the new offender. At this point, you ask **yourself** questions about the offender's apparent physical, mental, and emotional condition. The Health Screening Form contains basic medical questions because undetected and untreated medical problems heighten a person's anxiety which, in turn, can lead to suicide. Take a look again at the questions you will ask yourself, especially the highlighted questions that relate to identifying suicidal behavior.

Admissions Worker's Observations	Yes	No
3. Does the subject have any injury, or is he or she in any pain?	_____	_____
4. Does the subject have any signs of infection?	_____	_____
5. Does the subject appear to be under the influence of alcohol and/or drugs?	_____	_____
6. Does the subject have any signs of alcohol and/or drug withdrawal?	_____	_____
7. Does the subject appear to be suicidal?	_____	_____
Does the subject have wrist/neck scars?	_____	_____
8. Does the subject appear to be mentally ill?	_____	_____
9. Does the subject's behavior suggest risk of assault?	_____	_____
10. Does the subject appear to be mentally retarded?	_____	_____
11. Is the subject small, frail, seemingly weak?	_____	_____
12. Does the subject appear to be effeminate?	_____	_____
13. Does the subject appear to be naive, unsophisticated?	_____	_____
14. Is the subject carrying medication?	_____	_____

Your answers to the questions above are based upon your observations of the offender. Once again, be sure to follow up any "Yes" responses by writing specific information in the "Remarks" section at the end of the form.

QUESTIONS

How are medical problems related to suicide?

_____

_____

(1)

When you observe a new offender, you should try to assess his or her

_____ , _____ , and

_____ conditions.

(19)

Observing the New Offender (continued)

Although questioning yourself is the second step of the screening process, you may observe the offender (for screening purposes) at any time during the admissions process. For example, you may observe the new offender while he or she is taking a shower or changing clothes. However, before you proceed, make sure that you will be complying with your facility's policies and procedures for observing offenders—especially if the offender is a member of the opposite sex.

Note: In particular, you should look for signs of previous suicide attempts or the presence of factors that indicate the person is, or perhaps could become, suicidal.

> Make sure that you will be complying with your facility's policies and procedures for observing offenders.

For example, neck and wrist scars might indicate prior suicide attempts. And needle marks might indicate a history of drug abuse—a sign of potentially suicidal behavior.

Q

QUESTIONS

When you're observing an offender, what should you be looking for?

_____

_____

_____

_____

(13)

Step 3: Asking the Offender Questions

The third step of the screening process is asking the offender questions about his or her physical, mental, and emotional condition. Note again the questions you will be asking during the interview, especially the highlighted ones that relate to suicide prevention.

Admissions Worker/Subject Questions

Note: Before asking any questions, please say: "I am going to ask you some questions now. We ask these same questions of everybody who comes here because we're interested in their health and welfare."

	Yes	No	Refused to Answer
15. Are you presently taking any medication?	_____	_____	_____
If *yes*, for what? _____			
What type of medication? _____			
16. Do you use alcohol?	_____	_____	_____
If *yes*, how often? _____			
How much do you drink? _____			
When were you drunk last? _____			
When did you last take a drink? _____			
17. Do you use any street drugs?	_____	_____	_____
If *yes*, what type(s)? _____			
How often do you take drugs? _____			
When did you last take drugs? _____			
When were you high last? _____			
18. Is this the first time you have ever been confined?	_____	_____	_____
19. Have you ever thought about or attempted to commit suicide? _____	_____	_____	
Are you *now* concerned that you might attempt to commit suicide? _____			
20. Do you have any medical or mental problems now?	_____	_____	_____
If *yes*, are you receiving any treatment for the problems?	_____	_____	_____
If *yes*, what is the treatment? _____			
21. Have you had any previous mental or emotional problems? _____	_____	_____	
If *yes*, were you ever hospitalized for those problems?	_____	_____	_____
22. If the subject is *female*, ask:			
Are you pregnant?	_____	_____	_____
If *yes*, how many months? _____			
23. Are you on any special diet?	_____	_____	_____
If *yes*, what kind of diet is it and why are you on it? _____			
24. Is there anything special that we should know about you for your welfare or protection?	_____	_____	_____
If yes, what? _____			

Asking the Offender Questions (continued)

How you conduct the interview will determine whether you get good, honest responses. The guidelines below are designed to help you conduct a successful interview. By following these guidelines, you can expect to get honest answers about 90 percent of the time.

- Conduct the interview in as private a setting as possible. The more private the setting, the better the interview is likely to be.

- Explain what you are doing in simple terms. For example: "I'm going to ask you some questions about your health. We ask everyone these questions because we're interested in their health and welfare."

  This approach reduces the offender's feeling that he is being "picked on." Also, it conveys your "caring attitude" toward him.

- Ask questions in a common-sense, straightforward manner.

- Speak in a quiet, normal, matter-of-fact tone.

- Use language that the offender understands. For example, rather than say, "Have you ever *contemplated* suicide," say, "Have you ever *thought* about committing suicide or killing yourself."

- Repeat questions clearly and slowly if the offender does not understand them the first time.

- Avoid rushing, being abrupt, or being sarcastic.

Note: Asking an offender questions about suicide will not "plant" ideas in his or her head. Instead, asking such questions shows that you care about the offender's health and welfare.

Q

QUESTIONS

To interview an offender successfully, you should:

- Explain what you are doing in _____ terms

- Ask questions in a _____ and as _____ as possible

- Speak in a _____ tone

- Use _____ that the _____ understands

- Repeat questions _____, if the offender does not understand them the first time

- Avoid _____, being _____, or being
_____

(5)

Asking an offender questions about suicide will/will not (circle one) "plant" ideas in his or her head.

(10)

Step 4: Making a Disposition/Referral

The fourth step of the screening process is making a disposition or referral. This step involves deciding what to do with all the information you have gathered; it will be your most difficult screening task.

To complete this step, you should follow your facility's policies and procedures for making a disposition/referral. And, be sure you fill out the "Disposition or Referral" section of the Health Screening Form. Your facility's disposition or referral options will be similar to the ones listed on the form below.

> *Making a disposition involves deciding what to do with all the information you have gathered.*

DISPOSITION OR REFERRAL TO: (Please check applicable response):*

_____ Emergency care (state where): _____

_____ General population

_____ Close supervision, e.g., potential same-sex rape victim

_____ Sick call

_____ Placed in two-person cell or room (_____) (for communicable disease cases)

_____ Placed in suicide-resistant observation cell/room under constant supervision (high-risk suicide case)

_____ Placed in two- or more person cell/room or dormitory (_____) under special/close observation (suicidal offender)

NOTE: All these responses require documented action (i.e., state the basis for your disposition in the Remarks section). Follow your facility's "Guidelines for Disposition."

Your facility should have its own disposition checklist that reflects its resources and procedures. This checklist merely shows a sample approach that follows recognized practices.

A good rule to follow when assessing an offender is to **err on the side of caution**. This rule holds true especially when you're assessing an offender's suicide potential. For example, you should be sure to:

- Take all suicide threats seriously, including the **ninth** "wolf cry." Do not be judgmental and say, "Just ignore him. He's faking again." Do not drop or fail to carry out the proper suicide precautions. Many suicides occur because correctional workers fail to take repeated threats of suicide seriously. Many offenders who *seem* to manipulate for secondary gains do kill themselves. Staff who *manage* the offender as just a manipulator can incur heavy liability if the offender kills himself.

  Remember, you must respond to each suicide threat or attempt as the *first* threat or attempt.

- Try to "measure" the intensity of the offender's stress and depression. For example, is the offender *unusually* agitated? Does he show several signs and symptoms of depression?

- Determine the offender's impulsiveness. Remember that younger offenders are often more impulsive. For example, does the offender have a *history* of acting on *impulse* rather than *thought*?

When assessing an offender, you should err on the side of _____.

(9)

QUESTIONS

Making a Disposition/Referral (continued)

- Explore the offender's suicide potential and any plans he or she has for committing suicide by asking direct questions.

- Determine the means available to the offender to carry out his or her suicide plan, and remove these means whenever possible. This does not include stripping offenders naked, which worsens depression and shame. Such a practice is prohibited in systems where *positive* interventions exist. Suicidal offenders should not be subjected to substandard living conditions. If you do this, the offender may not disclose his suicidal intentions. Instead, he may "get well fast" and then attempt suicide later when the opportunity arises.

- Assess the resources available to prevent a suicide. Suicide prevention experts recommend that you should make a mental health referral in all cases of potential risk. Erring on the side of caution means reporting any offender who shows one or more signs and symptoms of suicidal behavior. Refer him to the appropriate staff, according to your facility's policies and procedures.

Your facility probably has developed a way for you to refer potentially suicidal offenders for assistance and observation. If it doesn't, you should ask your supervisor how to handle this situation.

Q

QUESTIONS

When assessing an offender's suicide potential, you should be sure to:

- Take _____ suicide threats seriously

- Try to "measure" the _____ of the offender's stress and depression

- Determine the offender's _____

- Explore the offender's _____and his or her plans for committing suicide by _____

- Determine the _____to the offender to carry out his or her suicide plan

- Assess the resources available to _____ a suicide

- Not subject him/her to _____ living conditions

(16)

You should make a mental health referral in _____ cases of suicide risk.

(3)

Making a Disposition/Referral (continued)

Sometimes, your assessment of an offender's suicide potential may differ from that of mental health staff. As a correctional worker, you "live with" the offender many hours per day while supervising him. This time factor may place you in a better position than anyone to truly assess suicide risk. Suppose you believe an offender is suicidal, but the mental health staff believe that he is not suicidal. What should you do?

Suppose you believe an offender is suicidal, but the mental health staff believe that he is not.

The best course of action is to *trust your own judgment*. If you believe an offender is in danger of committing suicide, listen to your "gut feelings." Act on your own beliefs. Don't let others mislead you into ignoring signs of potentially suicidal behavior. Talk with your supervisor about what to do. At the very least, you can watch the offender and document any potentially suicidal behavior.

Conversely, you should *abide by* mental health staff recommendations when they say an offender *is* suicidal.

When you believe that an offender is suicidal, but mental health staff disagree with your assessment, you should:

_____ A. Follow the recommendations of mental health staff

_____ B. Seek the advice of a fellow worker

_____ C. Note your beliefs on the Health Screening Form and let your supervisor decide what to do

_____ D. Trust your own judgment and talk with your supervisor about what to do

(7)

Medical Clearance

If a new offender is in need of immediate medical/psychiatric attention, the admissions worker must send the offender to the hospital or mental health facility for health clearance. A trained arresting or transportation officer usually will take the arrestee to the hospital directly for medical clearance. However, if the offender is taken to the jail first and refused admission, the arresting or transportation officer is expected to obtain the health clearance—because he or she still has jurisdiction over the arrestee. The officer must escort the offender to and from the hospital.

A physician or other qualified health professional* is responsible for medically assessing the offender. If the physician deems the offender healthy enough for detention, the offender is then "cleared" for admission into the facility. The physician simply fills out and signs the Health Clearance Form provided by the officer. In most cases, local forms will be used and will be similar to the sample on page 81.

The arresting or transportation officer gives the Health Clearance Form to the admissions worker after returning to the facility with the offender. **Under no circumstances should you admit an offender without the signed form.**

Q

QUESTIONS

The Health Clearance Form is filled out by the:

_____ A. Arresting officer

_____ B. Offender

_____ C. Physician or other qualified health professional

_____ D. Admissions worker

(18)

An arresting officer arrives at your facility with an offender who is in need of immediate medical attention. You should:

_____ A. Summon a doctor to your facility

_____ B. Ask the arresting or transportation officer to send the offender to the hospital or mental health facility for clearance

_____ C. Make note of the offender's condition and call your supervisor

_____ D. Medically assess the offender

(12)

Qualified health personnel are licensed, registered, and/or certified.

Mental Health Clearance

Assessing whether an offender is mentally suitable for admission is often more difficult than assessing his or her physical condition. But such a determination *can* and *must* be done.

An admissions worker should immediately send any offender who was recently a patient at a mental health facility, or who appears to be mentally ill, to a mental health professional for an assessment. Signs of mental illness include:

- Hears voices

- Behaves erratically

- Shows signs of suicidal behavior—especially if the offender says that he or she has suicidal thoughts

The mental health professional is responsible for assessing the mental health of the offender. If this professional deems the offender mentally suitable for admission, the offender is then "cleared" for admission into the facility. The mental health professional simply fills out and signs the Health Clearance Form provided by you.

Note: Generally, as an admissions worker, you should not admit a new offender who appears to be mentally ill or suicidal. If you are forced by policy or conditions to admit a mentally ill/suicidal offender, immediately notify your supervisor.

QUESTIONS

Mental health assessments are done in:

____ A. The facility

____ B. The community

____ C. Either the facility or the community

(2)

Medical Clearance (continued)

Depending on the size and location of the facility, the mental health professional may be on staff or a worker from a community agency. If the offender is to be assessed by someone outside the facility (perhaps at a local hospital), a trained arresting or transportation officer should escort the offender to and from the appointment.

The arresting or transportation officer gives the Health Clearance Form to the admissions worker after returning to the facility with the offender. **Under no circumstances should you admit an offender without the signed form.**

QUESTIONS

If a new offender appears mentally ill, you should:

____ A. Admit the offender and place him or her in isolation

____ B. Send the offender to a mental health professional for an assessment

____ C. Commit the offender to a state mental hospital

____ D. Mentally assess the offender

(8)

Health Clearance Form

Name of Subject† _____

Brought into Facility by _____

Date_____ Time_____

We have declined to accept the above-named subject into this facility, pending health clearance for the following reason(s):

_____

_____

_____

_____

_____   _____   _____

Signature of Worker   Date   Time

NAME OF EXAMINING PHYSICIAN*_____

DISPOSITION: _____   I have examined subject and find him/her **acceptable** for admission to the facility.

(Check one choice)   I have no specific suggestions about the care of this person concerning the condition for which I have examined him/her.

_____   I have examined subject and find him/her **acceptable** for admission into the facility.

I suggest treatment for subject's condition as described below.

_____   I have examined subject and find him/her **acceptable** for admission to the facility provided certain conditions are met, as described below.

_____   I have examined subject and find him/her **unacceptable** for admission to the facility.

PHYSICIAN'S REMARKS:

_____

_____

_____

_____

_____

_____   _____   _____   _____

Signature of Worker   Date   Time   Telephone number

†The term "subject" is used on this form instead of arrestee, inmate, or juvenile.

*Or qualified health professional

Summary

This chapter reviewed the initial health screening and clearance processes. It examined how to conduct a proper health screening of a newly admitted offender. In particular, it focused on how to conduct an effective interview with the offender. It also discussed the medical and mental health clearances.

1. Identify the four parts of a health screening.

   - All national standards require offenders to be assessed for medical and mental health fitness **upon arrival** at the facility.

   - Correctional workers can effectively do a *preliminary screening* or assessment of the offender's health. This assessment includes identifying the signs and symptoms of suicide. However, the medical and mental health *clearances* must be done by qualified professionals.

   - The first crucial high-risk period for suicide is during the first 24 hours of incarceration. Properly trained admissions workers can detect potentially suicidal offenders about 90 percent of the time at the initial health screening.

   - The health screening consists of four parts:

     — Asking the arresting or transportation officer questions

     — Observing the new offender

       When you observe a new offender, you should try to assess his or her physical, mental, and emotional conditions.

     — Asking the offender questions

     — Making a disposition or referral based on the information gathered during the screening process

2. Identify six conditions for which medical and mental health clearance should be required before admitting an arrestee into custody.

   - Injury

   - Infection

   - Under the influence of alcohol/drugs

   - Alcohol and/or drug withdrawal

   - Suicidal signs and symptoms

   - Mental illness

   - Mental retardation

3. List at least four observational questions related to identifying suicidal behavior.

   - Does the subject have any injury, or is she or he in any pain?

   - Does the subject appear to be under the influence of alcohol and/or drugs?

   - Does the subject have any signs of alcohol and/or drug withdrawal?

   - Does the subject appear to be suicidal?

   - Does the subject have wrist/neck scars?

   - Does the subject appear to be mentally ill?

4. List at least four interview questions related to identifying suicidal behavior.

   - Do you use alcohol?

     If yes, how often?

     How much do you drink?

     When were you drunk last?

     When did you last take a drink?

   - Do you use any street drugs?

     If yes, what types?

     How often do you take drugs?

When were you high last?

When did you last take drugs?

- Is this the first time you have ever been confined?

- Have you ever thought about or attempted to commit suicide?

  Are you *now* concerned that you might attempt to commit suicide?

- Do you have any medical or mental problems now?

  If yes, are you receiving any treatment for the problem?

  If yes, what is the treatment?

- Have you had any previous mental or emotional problems?

  If yes, were you ever hospitalized for those problems?

- If the subject is female, ask:

  Are you pregnant?

  If yes, how many months?

- Is there anything special that we should know about you for your welfare or protection?

  If yes, what?

5. List at least four guidelines for conducting a successful health screening interview.

- Conduct it in as private a setting as possible

- Explain what you are doing in simple terms

- Ask questions in a common-sense manner and as privately as possible

- Speak in a quiet, normal, matter-of-fact tone

- Use language that the offender understands

- Repeat questions clearly and slowly if the offender does not understand them the first time

- Avoid rushing, being abrupt, or being sarcastic

6. Identify six guidelines for making an appropriate disposition or referral.

- Err on the side of caution.

- Take all suicide threats seriously, including the ninth "wolf cry." Many offenders who seem to manipulate for secondary gains do kill themselves.

- Try to "measure" the intensity of the offender's stress and depression.

- Determine the offender's impulsiveness. Remember that younger offenders often have greater impulsiveness.

- Explore the offender's suicide potential and any plans he or she has for committing suicide by asking direct questions.

- Determine the means available to the offender to carry out his or her suicide plan, and remove these means whenever possible; however, do not subject the offender to substandard living conditions.

- Assess the resources available to *prevent* a suicide. Suicide prevention experts recommend that you should make a mental health referral in all cases of potential risk.

When you believe that an offender is suicidal, but mental health staff disagree with your assessment, you should trust your own judgment. Ask your supervisor what to do.

Answer Key—Assessing Suicide Risk: The Initial Health Screening and Clearance

1. Untreated medical problems heighten a person's anxiety which, in turn, can lead to suicide.

2. Mental health assessments are done in:

    _____ A. The facility

    _____ B. The community

    __✓__ C. Either the facility or the community

3. You should make a mental health referral in **all** cases of suicide risk.

4. Offenders might talk to arresting or transportation officers to relieve anxiety about an arrest or pending confinement.

5. To be successful in interviewing an offender, you should:

    • Explain what you are doing in **simple** terms

    • Ask questions in a **common-sense manner** and as **privately** as possible

    • Speak in a **quiet, normal, matter-of-fact** tone

    • Use **language** that the **offender** understands

    • Repeat questions **clearly and slowly**, if the offender does not understand them the first time

    • Avoid **rushing**, being **abrupt**, or being **sarcastic**

6. The first crucial high-risk period for suicide is during the first **24 hours** of incarceration.

7. When you believe that an offender is suicidal, but mental health staff disagree with your assessment, you should:

    _____ A. Follow the recommendations of mental health staff

    _____ B. Seek the advice of a fellow worker

    _____ C. Note your beliefs on the Health Screening Form and let your supervisor decide what to do

    __✓__ D. Trust your own judgment and talk with your supervisor about what to do

8. If a new offender appears mentally ill, you should:

    _____ A. Admit the offender and place him or her in isolation

    __✓__ B. Send the offender to a mental health professional for an assessment

    _____ C. Commit the offender to a state mental hospital

    _____ D. Mentally assess the offender

9. When assessing an offender, you should err on the side of **caution.**

10. Asking an offender questions about suicide **will not** "plant" ideas in his or her head.

11. The four parts of the Health Screening Form are:

    - Asking the arresting or transportation officer questions
    - Observing the new offender
    - Asking the offender questions
    - Making a disposition/referral, based on the information gathered during the screening process

12. An arresting officer arrives at your facility with an offender who is in need of immediate medical attention. You should:

    _____ A. Summon a doctor to your facility

    ✓ B. Ask the arresting or transportation officer to send the offender to the hospital or mental health facility for clearance

    _____ C. Make note of the offender's condition and call your supervisor

    _____ D. Medically assess the offender

13. When observing an offender, you should look for signs of previous suicide attempts or the presence of factors that indicate the offender is, or perhaps could become, suicidal.

14. All national standards require that facilities determine the medical and mental health fitness of **new** offenders upon arrival at the facility.

15. **True**. You should ask the arresting/transportation officer directly if the offender appeared to be suicidal or appeared to have other health problems.

16. When assessing an offender's suicide potential, you should be sure to:

    - Take **all** suicide threats seriously
    - Try to "measure" the **intensity** of the offender's stress and depression
    - Determine the offender's **impulsiveness**
    - Explore the offender's **suicide potential** and his or her plans for committing suicide by **asking direct questions**
    - Determine the **means available** to the offender to carry out his or her suicide plan
    - Assess the resources available to **prevent** a suicide
    - Not subject him/her to **substandard** living conditions

17. After you answer "Yes" to a question on the Health Screening Form, you should:

   ____ A. Write notes in the margin next to the question

   ____ B. Proceed directly to the next question

   ✓ C. Write down the specifics under the "Remarks" section

   ____ D. Tell the offender about it

18. The Health Clearance Form is filled out by the:

   ____ A. Arresting officer

   ____ B. Offender

   ✓ C. Physician or other qualified health professional

   ____ D. Admissions worker

19. When you observe a new offender, you should try to assess his or her **physical, mental,** and **emotional** conditions.

20. Match the common symptoms with their corresponding medical/psychological illnesses.

   1. Injury
   2. Infection
   3. Under the influence of alcohol/drugs
   4. Alcohol and/or drug withdrawal
   5. Suicide signs and symptoms
   6. Mental illness
   7. Mental retardation

   _7_ A. Slowness in reacting/understanding

   _5_ B. Depression

   _3_ C. Slurred speech

   _6_ D. Hearing voices

   _7_ E. Language problems

   _1_ F. Significant bleeding

   _2_ G. Yellow skin

   _4_ H. Severe shaking

   _6_ I. Erratic behavior

   _2_ J. Chronic cough/phlegm

CHAPTER SEVEN

Managing Potentially Suicidal Offenders

Objectives

At the end of this chapter, you will be able to:

1. List at least 12 of the principles of good discipline, custody, and mental health that influence suicide prevention.

2. Identify at least eight techniques for managing suicidal and mentally ill offenders.

Introduction

Correctional workers must have good interpersonal communication skills to prevent suicides. It often seems that certain workers are born with these skills. They are "naturals" in our field. They automatically follow the Golden Rule: treat others as you want to be treated. They know intuitively how to interact with others in a way that achieves positive results.

Most of us, however, must learn to be effective in our communications. We must learn to be effective in human interaction. We must learn to be effective correctional workers.

Effective correctional workers practice the "Do's and Don'ts" of good discipline, custody, and mental health. They are true *team* workers. They do a good job of identifying and managing suicidal offenders. In addition, these workers help minimize other problems by creating a better overall atmosphere in the facility.

This chapter will identify the "Do's and Don'ts" of good discipline, custody, and mental health that influence suicide prevention. The chapter also will identify techniques for effectively managing potentially suicidal offenders.

"Do's and Don'ts" of Good Discipline, Custody, and Mental Health

The following "Do's and Don'ts" of good offender management are based on interviews with several thousand correctional workers throughout the United States. They influence not only suicide prevention efforts but also the operations of the facility. Most correctional professionals agree that effective correctional workers follow these guidelines.

Do's

- Be fair

  Fairness in workers is ranked highest among all attributes. Follow the same practices with all offenders.

- Keep promises

  Broken promises are lies to offenders; staff who break promises are despised by fellow staff who must later deal with the disgruntled offenders.

- Use power and authority positively
  - —See that the sanction or discipline fits the infraction
  - —Refer more often to "we" than to "I" or "me"
  - —Do not stress "I'm in charge; you listen to me"

- Admit mistakes

  The worker who admits his or her mistakes is elevated, not lowered in the eyes of others.

- Answer legitimate questions

  Some workers don't or won't answer appropriate questions; or, when they do, frequently counter with, "Why do you want to know?" or "What business is it of yours?" Failure to answer legitimate questions breaks down good officer-offender communications. If you must refuse to answer questions that deal with security or other sensitive issues, you should be courteous.

- Ask—rather than order—that something be done

  Workers most respected by offenders generally ask instead of order that something be done. Asking shows respect and creates a feeling of ownership in decision making; it also leads to better cooperation. If asking doesn't work, you can give an order.

- Be consistent

  Both offenders and fellow officers view consistency as being one of the most desired traits of good workers.

- Talk with offenders

  Talking with offenders about legitimate matters produces better staff-offender relationships.

- Be looked up to as role models

  Inmates often look for good role models, an important factor in rehabilitation.

- Be a team worker

  Many inmates are quick to pick out the "loner" or non-team member.

- Be self-confident, not arrogant

  Self-confident workers positively sell only what they can deliver. The arrogant person oversells, often in an overbearing manner.

- Demonstrate sincerity and honesty
  - —Keep commitments
  - —Give factual answers
  - —Listen attentively
  - —Talk with offenders about their concerns
  - —Say "I don't know" when asked a question you can't answer, and then try to find out the answer, or direct the offender to someone who can answer the question

- Give credit where credit is due—seek out positives

  Some supervisors constantly look for things that go wrong; instead, supervisors should be devoted to seeking out *positives,* an approach increasingly stressed in business and industry. Likewise, you should do the same when dealing with offenders.

- Accept constructive criticism

  In order to improve their own performances, some correctional workers seek constructive criticism from their superiors and others, and accept responsibility for their mistakes without trying to make excuses.

- Have an open mind

  Effective correctional workers actively seek new ideas or better ways of doing things, or, when such ideas are presented, they fully consider them.

- Leave personal problems at home; keep personal problems to yourself

  Offenders recognize those staff who come to work "bent out of shape" due to psycho-logical or family problems, excessive drinking, or other reasons. It is difficult to earn respect from offenders under this circumstance. The same holds true for sharing personal problems with offenders. Keep your problems to yourself. Otherwise, offenders may use the information to try to manipulate you.

- Do more than what is expected

  The "average" worker generally will not make the top quarter of the ratings list. As someone once said, "Two percent extra effort can make 100 percent difference."

- Be patient

  Patient staff are secure, self-confident workers who follow the Golden Rule.

- Have a caring attitude

  This trait is frequently mentioned because of the contrast between staff who "care," and those who put themselves first and others second. Experts stress that "If only one person *cares* and *shows* a caring attitude, the suicide most likely will not occur."

Q

QUESTIONS

List two ways you can use authority positively.

- _____
- _____

(6)

List three ways you can show offenders that you're sincere and honest.

- _____
- _____
- _____

(2)

True/ False   Effective workers answer all the questions asked by offenders.

(9)

"Do's and Don'ts" of Good Discipline, Custody, and Mental Health (continued)

Don'ts

- Do not show favoritism

  When correctional workers show *favoritism* among offenders or staff, peers say *it is not fair*.

  For example, do not have "favorite" offenders that you treat differently than other offenders.

- Do not use put-downs

  For example, do not make critical statements such as:

  —"Who are you to speak?"

  —"I'm on this side of the bars; you're on the other side."

  —"You're not very smart, or you wouldn't be in here."

- Do not criticize staff in front of others

  For example, avoid damaging remarks, such as:

  —"When Officer Jones is on, she can do it her way. But I don't think like she does."

  —"Mondays are hard days for Officer Jackson; humor him that day."

- Do not constantly threaten offenders

  Like many parents, some correctional workers keep threatening, and offenders soon learn that a great deal of it is bluff; this results in poor respect and poor discipline. Remember that good behavior is best shown through example—through being a role model—not through frequent commands.

- Do not withdraw support from offenders who resist help

  The correctional worker who doesn't easily give up on an offender—even when the offender resists help—may help create positive change in that offender's life. Not giving up conveys the feeling that "someone cares" and can be a key factor in preventing a suicide.

- Do not preach

  Offenders generally resist and resent "preachy," judgmental correctional workers.

- Do not yell or swear

  Some workers defend this on the grounds that "that's all the inmates know." However, such language means getting down to the offenders' level, not serving as a much needed role model.

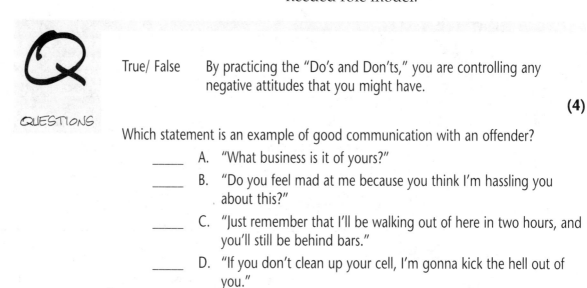

True/ False   By practicing the "Do's and Don'ts," you are controlling any negative attitudes that you might have.

(4)

Which statement is an example of good communication with an offender?

_____ A. "What business is it of yours?"

_____ B. "Do you feel mad at me because you think I'm hassling you about this?"

_____ C. "Just remember that I'll be walking out of here in two hours, and you'll still be behind bars."

_____ D. "If you don't clean up your cell, I'm gonna kick the hell out of you."

(7)

Managing Suicidal and Mentally Ill Offenders

To manage suicidal and mentally ill offenders effectively, you will need some special techniques. Some of the things you can do are:

- Try to **calm** the individual and reduce his or her anxiety by being calm, firm, fair, reasonable, and confident. For example: "Can you tell me what concerns you have?"

Explain:

—How you see the problem

—What is being done

—What the outcome will be

To manage suicidal and mentally ill offenders effectively, you will need some special techniques.

For example: "I'll be glad to explain how the legal system operates. What questions do you have?"

- Explain that, from your experience, the crisis is just **temporary** and generally can be worked out.

Encourage the offender to:

—Speak freely

—Express any feelings

—Relate to you

For example: "Please tell me what bothers you most. We'll try to help you."

Q

QUESTIONS

To calm a person, you need to be _____, firm, fair, _____, and _____ .

(1)

When you talk with suicidal offenders, you should encourage them to _____ freely, _____ their feelings, and _____ to you.

(3)

Managing Suicidal and Mentally Ill Offenders (continued)

- To facilitate the most effective handling of the suicidal offender, and to avoid affecting other offenders in the area, you should:

  —Remove the suicidal offender from the scene of the crisis (if possible), or

  —Lock down the cellblock, tier, or wing

- **Avoid** arguing. Do not belittle the offender's situation.

- **Help** the offender *structure* the experience so that:

  —It is not so chaotic

  —It does not appear unusual (help the offender "get hold of himself or herself")

  Structuring means helping the offender see the situation in a different, positive light. For example, you might say: "Many offenders feel the same way you do; it's a different kind of living in here. Give yourself time to adjust."

- **Do not:**

  —Speak sarcastically

  —Lie

  —Make promises you cannot keep

- **Trust** your own judgment. Don't let others mislead you when you feel the offender is suicidal. This includes mental health workers who say the offender is "not suicidal."

- **Stay** with the suicidal person, at least until help arrives.

- **Maintain** contact (presence) and continue the conversation.

- **Express** concern about the person.

- **Listen** patiently. REMEMBER: If you keep the offender talking, he or she probably will not commit suicide.

Q QUESTIONS

If you believe an offender is suicidal but a fellow worker doesn't, you should:

_____ A. Follow your fellow worker's judgment

_____ B. Follow your own judgment and talk with your supervisor

(10)

Which of these actions is an appropriate way to deal with an offender who is attempting to commit suicide?

_____ A. Telling the offender that committing suicide is stupid

_____ B. Reassuring the offender that "everything will be all right"

_____ C. Telling the offender that the crisis is temporary and can be worked out

_____ D. Promising the offender that you will get his or her sentence reduced

(5)

You can show an offender that you care by _____ contact (presence) and continuing the conversation, and by _____ concern.

(8)

Whenever you believe that **a risk of suicide exists**, you should contact mental health personnel. In many cases, however, this is not possible because 24-hour mental health services are not available. In this situation, you must continually observe the offender, or have the designated staff, or offender "companions," "buddies," or "watchers" do so. (We will discuss offender "companions" in Chapter 14.)

That is why line staff, who work with offenders 24 hours a day, must be the backbone of suicide detection and prevention, and why capable mental health personnel should be regarded as support services.

Indeed, properly trained correctional workers already have proven that they can detect and prevent most suicides.

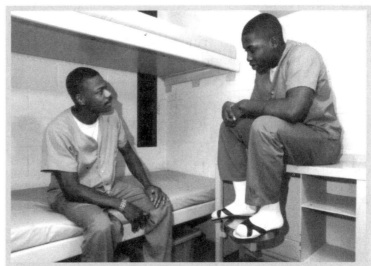

Who must be the backbone of suicide detection and prevention in custody?

_____ A. The administrator

_____ B. The supervisor

_____ C. The mental health professional

_____ D. The correctional officer or juvenile careworker

(11)

Summary

This chapter identified the "Do's and Don'ts" of good discipline, custody, and mental health that influence suicide prevention. The chapter also identified techniques for effectively managing potentially suicidal offenders.

1. List at least 12 of the principles of good discipline, custody, and mental health that influence suicide prevention.

   - The key to suicide prevention is human interaction by capable, properly trained staff.

   - Effective correctional workers practice the "Do's and Don'ts" of good discipline, custody, and mental health. They are true team workers. They do a good job identifying and managing suicidal people in custody.

     — Be fair

     — Keep promises

     — Use power and authority positively

     — Admit mistakes

     — Answer legitimate questions

     — Ask—rather than order—that something be done

     — Be consistent

     — Talk with offenders

     — Be looked up to as a role model

     — Be a team worker

     — Be self-confident

     — Demonstrate sincerity and honesty

     — Give credit where credit is due—seek out positives

     — Accept constructive criticism

     — Have an open mind

     — Leave personal problems at home; keep personal problems to yourself

     — Do more than what is expected

     — Be patient

     — Have a caring attitude

2. Identify at least eight techniques for managing suicidal and mentally ill offenders.

   - You, the line worker, must be the backbone of suicide detection and prevention. Mental health workers provide important support services.

     — Try to calm the offender and reduce his or her anxiety by being calm, firm, fair, reasonable, and confident.

     — Explain how you see the problem, what is being done, and what the outcome will be.

     — Explain that from your experience, the crisis is just temporary and generally can be worked out.

     — Encourage the offender to speak freely, express any feelings, and relate to you.

     — Avoid arguing.

     — Help the offender structure the experience so that it is not chaotic, and it doesn't appear unusual. Structuring means helping the offender see the situation in a different, positive light.

     — Do not speak sarcastically, lie, and/or make promises you cannot keep.

     — Trust your own judgement.

     — Stay with the suicidal person, at least until help arrives.

     — Maintain contact (presence) and continue the conversation.

     — Express concern about the person.

     — Listen patiently. If you keep the offender talking he probably will not commit suicide.

Answer Key—Managing Potentially Suicidal Offenders

1. To calm a person, you need to be **calm**, firm, fair, **reasonable**, and **confident**.

2. Ways you can show offenders that you're sincere and honest are: (choose three)

   - Keep your commitments

   - Give factual answers

   - Listen attentively

   - Talk with offenders about their concerns

   - Say "I don't know" when asked a question you can't answer, and then find out the answer, or refer the offender to someone who can answer the question

3. When you talk with suicidal offenders, you should encourage them to **speak** freely, **express** their feelings, and **relate** to you.

4. **True**. By practicing the "Do's and Don'ts," you avoid expressing negative attitudes that may cloud your ability to detect signs and symptoms of suicidal behavior.

5. An appropriate way to deal with an offender who is attempting to commit suicide is by:

   _____ A. Telling the offender that committing suicide is stupid

   _____ B. Reassuring the offender that "everything will be all right"

   _✓_ C. Telling the offender that the crisis is temporary and can be worked out

   _____ D. Promising the offender that you will get his or her sentence reduced

6. Ways you can use authority positively are: (choose two)

   - See that the sanction or discipline fits the infraction

   - Refer more often to "we" than to "I" or "me"

   - Do not stress "I'm in charge; you listen to me"

7. This statement is an example of good communication with an offender:

   _____ A. "What business is it of yours?"

   _✓_ B. "Do you feel mad at me because you think I'm hassling you about this?"

   _____ C. "Just remember that I'll be walking out of here in two hours, and you'll still be behind bars."

   _____ D. "If you don't clean up your cell, I'm gonna kick the hell out of you."

8. You can show an offender that you care by **maintaining** contact (presence) and continuing the conversation, and by **expressing** concern.

9. **False.** Effective workers answer **legitimate** questions. They refuse to answer—in a courteous manner—questions about security or other sensitive issues.

10. If you believe an offender is suicidal but a fellow worker, even mental health staff, doesn't, you should:

    _____ A. Follow your fellow worker's judgment

    _✓_ B. Follow your own judgment and talk with your supervisor

11. The person who must be the backbone of suicide detection and prevention in custody is:

    _____ A. The administrator

    _____ B. The supervisor

    _____ C. The mental health professional

    _✓_ D. The correctional officer or juvenile careworker

CHAPTER EIGHT

The Role of the Correctional Worker in Suicide Prevention

Objectives

At the end of this chapter, you will be able to:

1. Identify the five duties a correctional worker has in preventing suicides.

2. Identify the five guidelines that outline a correctional worker's role in preventing suicides.

Introduction

Correctional officers or juvenile careworkers play the most important role in preventing suicides. They are considered to be the backbone of suicide prevention. To fulfill their role, they must perform a variety of duties. One of their most important duties is to use good interpersonal communication skills, which we discussed in the previous chapter. These skills enable officers to identify and manage suicidal offenders effectively.

This chapter will review the duties of the correctional worker in preventing suicides in custody. The chapter also will outline the correctional worker's role in carrying out these duties.

Role of the Direct Service Worker

As a correctional worker, your duties related to suicide prevention include: using good interpersonal communication skills; accurately documenting offender behavior; making various dispositions; referring offenders to your supervisor and/or to mental health services; and encouraging the offenders to participate in them.

John P. Finnerty, in *Suicide Prevention in Correctional Facilities*, best outlined your role in preventing suicides. He said:

BE AWARE of the symptoms ordinarily displayed by an offender prior to a suicide attempt. Courts expect correctional workers to be able to *foresee* what may happen when certain signs and symptoms of suicidal behavior appear.

BE TUNED IN to the obvious and sometimes subtle signals that almost every suicidal offender sends out. Failure to do this because of a supposed "lack of time" is no defense in a lawsuit. Controlling *negative* attitudes is essential for effective "tuning in."

HAVE DAILY CONTACT with offenders. Effectiveness is determined by how well you *listen* and *observe*.

BE EMPATHIC with offenders and do not judge them. You are responsible for the welfare of those offenders under your supervision, not for judging their moral character. Your *feelings* and *understanding* of what the offender is going through must be genuine and be perceived as such by the offender. It's a good idea to place yourself in the offender's shoes and imagine how you would feel.

Many of us often confuse the terms sympathy and empathy. *Sympathy* means **sharing** another person's feelings, such as sadness. In contrast, *empathy* means being **understanding** of the other person's feelings. Here are a few ways that you can show empathy:

- Tune into the offender's "radio channel," not yours. Show that you're listening and tuned in to *his* "channel" by making an empathic statement such as: "Can you tell me more about that?"

Q

QUESTIONS

How effective your contact with offenders will be in terms of preventing suicides depends on how well you _____ and
_____ .

(2)

The correctional _____ plays the most important role in suicide prevention.

(4)

You are responsible for _____ offender behavior.

(6)

Role of the Direct Service Worker (continued)

- Ask one question at a time. For example: "You said you've thought about killing yourself. When was the last time you felt that way?" Now pause and let the offender answer. Then you can ask, "What happened to make you feel that way?"

- Give simple responses and minimal encouragers to the offender's statements. This lets the offender know that your listening. Minimal encouragers are words and phrases that show you're listening. They include: "mmm-hmm," "oh?," "tell me more," "I see," "then?" Use them frequently in the early part of a conversation and infrequently later on. Let them flow naturally.

- Be silently attentive when appropriate. Listening is the major part of your job. It gives the offender time to talk at his own pace. You should listen when you sense it's appropriate to do so. You can show that you're being attentive by using a nonverbal gesture such as nodding your head.

NEVER GIVE UP on an offender. If he appears to resist help, do not be impulsive and withdraw your support. More often than not, an offender's resistance is superficial and will disappear gradually if you continue to be empathic and helpful.

By taking such actions, you may be able to prevent an unnecessary death.

QUESTIONS

True/False   To effectively prevent suicides, you must control your judgmental attitudes and dislike of certain offenders.

(1)

List five things correctional workers can do to detect and prevent suicides in custody.

- _____
- _____
- _____
- _____
- _____

(3)

Identify the difference between being sympathetic and being empathic. Then list two ways that you can show empathy toward an offender.

_____
_____
_____
_____

(5)

103

The Role of the Correctional Worker
in Suicide Prevention

Summary

This chapter reviewed the duties of the correctional worker in preventing suicides in custody. The chapter also outlined the correctional worker's role in carrying out these duties.

1. Identify the five duties a correctional worker has in preventing suicides.

   - Having good interpersonal communication skills

   - Documenting offender behavior

   - Making various dispositions

   - Referring an offender to his or her supervisor and/or mental health services

   - Encouraging an offender to participate in mental health services

2. Identify the five guidelines that outline a correctional worker's role in preventing suicides.

   - BE AWARE of the symptoms ordinarily displayed by an offender prior to a suicide attempt

   - BE TUNED IN to the obvious and sometimes subtle signals that almost every suicidal offender sends out

   - HAVE DAILY CONTACT with offenders

   - BE EMPATHIC with offenders and do not judge them

   - NEVER GIVE UP on an offender

Answer Key—The Role of the Correctional Worker in Suicide Prevention

1. **True.** To effectively prevent suicides, you must control your negative attitudes.

2. How effective your contact with offenders will be in terms of preventing suicides depends on how well you **listen** and **observe**.

3. Five things correctional workers can do to detect and prevent suicides in custody are:

    - BE AWARE of the symptoms ordinarily displayed by an offender prior to a suicide attempt
    - BE TUNED IN to the obvious and sometimes subtle signals that almost every suicidal offender sends out
    - HAVE DAILY CONTACT with offenders
    - BE EMPATHIC with offenders and do not judge them
    - NEVER GIVE UP on an offender

4. The correctional **worker** plays the most important role in suicide prevention.

5. *Sympathy* means **sharing** another person's feelings, such as sadness. In contrast, *empathy* means being **understanding** of the other person's feelings. Ways that you can show empathy toward an offender include:

    - Tune into the offender's "radio channel," not yours
    - Ask one question at a time
    - Give simple responses and minimal encouragers to the offender's statements
    - Be silently attentive when appropriate

6. Your are responsible for **documenting** offender behavior.

Suicides in Custody: Facts vs. Fiction

Objectives

At the end of this chapter, you will be able to:

1. Identify why misconceptions about suicide can have serious consequences in the correctional setting.

2. List at least five myths about suicides in custody and their accompanying facts.

Introduction

In the last chapter, we discussed the role of the correctional worker in preventing suicides. We learned that the key to preventing suicides is positive interaction and positive intervention. It's human nature, however, to have not only negative attitudes but also misconceptions. We hear something and believe it to be true.

In some cases, our misconceptions can have serious consequences. For example, many of us have misconceptions about suicide. In the correctional setting, these misconceptions can unintentionally lead to suicides. To effectively prevent suicides, you must learn what is fact and what is fiction. You must dispel the myths and correct your misconceptions.

Experts have designed a list of the most common misconceptions or myths about suicide. This chapter will identify each of these myths and their accompanying facts, and explain why the myths are false.

The Facts and the Fiction of Suicides in Custody

MYTH: People who make suicidal statements or threaten suicide don't commit suicide.

FACT: Most people who commit suicide have made either direct or indirect statements that indicate their suicidal intentions. Many suicides occur when staff often ignore repeated suicide threats because they view them as manipulative gestures. *Many manipulators kill themselves.*

EXPLANATION: Research has shown that of ten people who kill themselves, eight have given definite warnings of their suicidal intentions. These warnings may be direct statements: "I'm going to kill myself." Others may be more indirect statements: "You won't have to worry about me anymore," or "You'd be better off without me."

Offenders may make these statements in a serious, sarcastic, or even joking manner. They may make these statements to you, to relatives or friends, or even to other offenders. The point is that people planning to commit suicide often talk about their plans and feelings. *You should not ignore these signs.*

MYTH: Suicides occur suddenly and without warning.

FACT: Most suicides represent a carefully thought-out strategy for coping with serious personal problems. *Caution*: However, nearly one-third of suicide deaths in jails occur within *three* hours of admission. This is due in great part to offenders being incarcerated for the first time; thrust into a strange, authoritarian environment; and/or being under the influence of alcohol/drugs.

EXPLANATION: Studies reveal that suicidal persons give many clues and warnings about their intentions. It is particularly difficult within the correctional environment to attempt suicide on impulse. Offenders must carefully plan the best method and choose the opportune time.

Q

QUESTIONS

People planning to commit suicide often _____ about their plans and feelings.

(3)

An offender planning to commit suicide must carefully plan the best _____ and the _____.

(6)

CHAPTER 9
Suicides in Custody:
Facts vs. Fiction

110

The Facts and the Fiction of Suicides in Custody (continued)

MYTH: People who attempt suicide have gotten it out of their system and won't attempt it again.

FACT: Four out of five people who kill themselves have made at least one prior attempt.

EXPLANATION: If a person has made an attempt on his or her life, taboos against taking his or her life have been broken. Other attempts then become easier. Although some attempts may seem minor and merely attention-getting behavior, they are calls for help. If you ignore such calls, other more serious attempts are likely.

MYTH: Suicidal people want to die.

FACT: Most suicidal people have mixed feelings about killing themselves. They really do not know whether they want to live or die. Many, though, do want to live. They just want their problem to go away.

EXPLANATION: Most people give definite warnings of suicidal intentions. On some level, they wish to be saved. They may not want to die, but at that particular time, they see no other choice.

MYTH: You can't stop someone in custody who really wants to commit suicide.

FACT: Most suicidal persons want to be rescued. Therefore, most suicides in custody can be prevented.

EXPLANATION: Once again, most suicidal individuals wish to be saved. The stress factors bearing down on these individuals block their ability to see other, positive choices. In other words, they cannot see the "light at the end of the tunnel"; they only see the darkness of the tunnel.

Most suicidal persons want to be rescued. So most suicides in custody can be prevented.

Q

Most people who intend to commit suicide give definite _____ of _____ that are calls for help.

(1)

Most suicidal people have _____ about killing themselves.

(8)

111

CHAPTER 9
Suicides in Custody:
Facts vs. Fiction

MYTH: Asking offenders about suicidal thoughts or actions will cause them to kill themselves.

FACT: You cannot make people suicidal—or make them carry out their thoughts of suicide—when you show interest in their welfare.

EXPLANATION: Offenders will not get ideas of suicide—or get the courage to carry out their suicidal thoughts—by discussing the possibility of their committing suicide. *Asking* is perceived by many offenders as "caring." Sensing that "somebody cares" prevents some offenders from attempting suicide.

Q QUESTIONS

True/False   You never can stop offenders in custody from committing suicide if they really mean it.

(4)

True/False   Asking offenders if they have thought about suicide will give them the idea to do it.

(7)

CHAPTER 9
Suicides in Custody:
Facts vs. Fiction

112

MYTH: All suicidal individuals are mentally ill—they're insane.

FACT: Although suicidal persons are extremely unhappy and most likely depressed, they are not necessarily insane. Depression is a major sign of suicidal behavior. In fact, most suicide deaths in custody are preceded or accompanied by *situational* depression, which disappears when the situation is resolved. Few suicides in custody involve *clinical* or deep-seated depression. Although depression is a mental illness, persons who are depressed are not insane.

EXPLANATION: Many people believe that a person must be insane to commit suicide. However, studies of hundreds of suicide notes indicate otherwise. They show that, although the suicidal person is unhappy and depressed, he or she is not necessarily insane or psychotic—being out of touch with reality, behaving in a bizarre manner, or suffering from hallucinations. Thus, a "normal" person who is in touch with reality can be suicidal.

QUESTIONS

To prevent suicides, you must:

_____   A. Take *all* threats seriously

_____   B. Look for subtle and/or "silent" signs

_____   C. Ignore obvious manipulations by offenders

_____   D. Accept prior suicide attempts as predictors or signs

(2)

True/False   People who commit suicide are not normal; they must be insane.

(5)

113

CHAPTER 9
Suicides in Custody:
Facts vs. Fiction

Summary

Experts have designed a list of the most common misconceptions or myths about suicide. This chapter identified the most common myths about suicide and their accompanying facts, and explained why the myths are false.

1. Identify why misconceptions about suicide can have serious consequences in the correctional setting.

   - In the correctional setting, misconceptions about suicide can unintentionally lead to or foster suicides.

2. List at least five myths about suicides in custody and their accompanying facts.

   - In the correctional setting, myths or misconceptions about suicide can unintentionally lead to suicides. To effectively prevent suicides in custody, you must learn what is fact and what is fiction.

   - The most common myths about suicide and their accompanying facts are:

   MYTH: People who make suicidal statements or threaten suicide don't commit suicide.

   FACT: Most people who commit suicide have made either direct or indirect statements that indicate their suicidal intentions.

   MYTH: Suicides occur suddenly and without warning.

   FACT: Most suicides represent a carefully thought-out strategy for coping with serious personal problems. The exception are those suicides—one-third of all suicides in custody—that occur in jails within the first three hours of admission.

   MYTH: People who attempt suicide have gotten it out of their system and won't attempt it again.

   FACT: Four out of five people who kill themselves have made at least one prior attempt.

   MYTH: Suicidal people want to die.

   FACT: Most suicidal people have mixed feelings about killing themselves. They really do not know whether they want to live or die. Many, though, do want to live. They just want their problem to go away.

   MYTH: You can't stop someone in custody who really wants to commit suicide.

   FACT: Most suicidal persons want to be rescued. Therefore, almost all suicides in custody can be prevented.

   MYTH: Asking and probing offenders about suicidal thoughts or actions will cause them to kill themselves.

   FACT: You cannot make people suicidal—or make them carry out their thoughts of suicide—when you show interest in their welfare.

   MYTH: All suicidal individuals are mentally ill.

   FACT: Although suicidal persons are extremely unhappy and probably depressed, they are not necessarily insane.

CHAPTER 9
Suicides in Custody:
Facts vs. Fiction

114

Answer Key—Suicides in Custody: Facts vs. Fiction

1. Most people who intend to commit suicide give definite **warnings** of **suicidal intentions** that are calls for help.

2. To prevent suicides, you must:

    _✓_ A.   Take *all* threats seriously

    _✓_ B.   Look for subtle and/or "silent" signs

    ____ C.   Ignore obvious manipulation by offenders

    _✓_ D.   Accept prior suicide attempts as predictors or signs

3. People planning to commit suicide often **talk** about their plans and feelings.

4. **False**. Most suicidal persons want to be rescued. Therefore, most suicides in custody can be prevented.

5. **False**. People do not have to be insane or psychotic to commit suicide.

6. An offender planning to commit suicide must carefully plan the best **method** and the **opportune time**.

7. **False**. You cannot make offenders suicidal when you show interest in their welfare by discussing the possibility of their committing suicide.

8. Most suicidal people have **mixed feelings** about killing themselves.

Avoiding Liability in Suicide-Related Lawsuits

Objectives

At the end of this chapter, you will be able to:

1. Identify four ways correctional staff can avoid liability in suicide-related lawsuits.

2. Describe at least six parts of an effective suicide prevention plan.

3. Identify two guidelines for properly housing suicidal offenders.

Introduction

About ten years ago, lawsuits involving suicides in custody were unusual. Today, these lawsuits are common. An estimated eight out of ten suicides result in a lawsuit. As we mentioned in Chapter 1, family members often will question the care given to their loved ones and file suicide-related lawsuits. These lawsuits have a major bearing on suicide prevention in custody.

Similarly, 15 years ago, correctional workers were rarely named as defendants in suicide-related lawsuits. Today, however, this practice is common. This means that you must be able to prove that you carried out your suicide prevention duties effectively and lawfully.

This chapter will identify ways you can avoid liability in suicide-related lawsuits, and examine the key parts of an effective suicide prevention plan.

Avoiding Liability in Suicide-Related Lawsuits

Correctional workers can avoid liability in suicide-related lawsuits by following established policies, procedures, job descriptions, and professional training. "We-minded" team workers usually adhere to such practices. "I-me" workers, however, do not. They are self-centered, arrogant, and frequently unable to control their negative attitudes. These workers also tend to abuse authority. Thus, the "I-me" workers are most likely to be held liable in a suicide-related lawsuit.

One of the best ways to avoid liability is by following the procedures in your facility's suicide prevention plan. If your facility does not have such a plan, you should discuss developing one with your supervisor.

An effective suicide prevention plan includes procedures for:

Identification—identifying newly admitted offenders at receiving who are potentially suicidal. The *overall* health screening can help you accomplish this task.

Training—training all staff to detect and prevent suicides. You and your fellow workers must be trained to recognize both verbal and non-verbal (behavioral) clues of potentially suicidal behavior. Experts usually recommend *eight* hours of training in identifying and managing suicidal offenders, with refresher training at least every two years. The training should include how to conduct an effective health screening.

Q

QUESTIONS

To avoid liability, correctional workers must follow established:

- _____
- _____
- _____
- _____

(1)

Who is likely to be held liable in a lawsuit?

_____ A. "I-me" worker

_____ B. "We-minded" worker

_____ C. Team worker

_____ D. Both B and C

(5)

True/False   A good way to avoid liability is to follow your facility's suicide prevention plan.

(8)

True/False   Clues of potentially suicidal behavior can be verbal or non-verbal.

(12)

Assessment—assessing potentially suicidal offenders. You must be able, with the assistance of mental health professionals, to make decisions about potentially suicidal offenders whenever necessary. If mental health staff are not available, you should consult medical staff who have mental health training. (See Chapter 6, "Sample Health Screening Form.")

Monitoring—monitoring or supervising potentially suicidal offenders. You especially must know how intense the supervision should be.

Housing—You should **not** place potentially suicidal offenders in isolation unless you can **constantly** supervise them. If you cannot **constantly** supervise these offenders, then place them with two or more other selected and trained offenders. These "cellmates" can serve as companions—not staff—and call for help if an emergency arises. Companions are usually located outside the cell or room.

Under these conditions, you must supervise the potentially suicidal offenders **at least every ten minutes**.

If you place potentially suicidal offenders in suicide-resistant rooms, you need to supervise them every **three to four minutes** because some offenders do commit suicide in these settings by very "creative" techniques. It takes less than ten minutes for a successful suicide to occur.

You should also exercise extreme caution when monitoring an offender away from his cell/room. Suicide attempts often occur in bathrooms, stairwells, closets, and vacant rooms.

Note: Two-thirds of all suicides in custody occur in isolation.

Q

QUESTIONS

You should not place potentially suicidal offenders in isolation unless they can be _____ supervised—observed.

(2)

True/False   Offender companions relieve you of supervising potentially suicidal offenders so that you can carry out other duties.

(6)

If a potentially suicidal offender is in a suicide-resistant room, you must supervise him every _____ to _____ minutes.

(9)

Avoiding Liability in Suicide-Related Lawsuits (continued)

Referral—referring potentially suicidal offenders to mental health services. You should follow your facility's policies and procedures to carry out this duty properly. Be sure to document your actions.

If you have any questions about how to make a referral or are unsure what to do in a particular situation, talk things over with your supervisor.

Communication—communicate with other staff about potentially suicidal offenders. You should keep other staff—including mental health staff—informed both verbally and in writing of any current information about potentially suicidal offenders.

The "duty to warn" principle requires that mental health professionals must relay their opinions about an offender's suicide poten-

tial to correctional workers. This practice does NOT violate the offender's confidentiality in relation to mental health records. In fact, several state legislatures have mandated that this practice be followed.

Intervention—intervening to prevent suicides. You should take positive steps to prevent suicides, such as listening, questioning, and referring offenders to mental health services.

In addition, you should know how to respond to a suicide attempt. For example, you should know the method for quickly cutting down a hanging victim, as well as other immediate first-aid measures.

Q

QUESTIONS

You can prevent a suicide attempt or death by:

- _____
- _____
- _____
- _____

(3)

True/False   Mental health professionals cannot tell you their opinions about suicide potential for reasons of confidentiality.

(7)

True/False   Only medical staff should know how to respond to a suicide attempt because they are responsible for emergency care.

(10)

Notification—notifying officials, family members, and significant others about attempted or completed suicides.

Reporting—reporting and documenting attempted or completed suicides as required by law, administrative procedure, and/or agency policy.

Administrative Review—participating in the "administrative review," also known as a "psychological autopsy." (This topic will be covered in Chapter 13.)

When a *completed suicide* or actual *attempt* occurs, your facility's administrators should conduct an "administrative review" of the events surrounding the tragedy. This practice is essential in preventing the next attempted or completed suicide, and for preventing potential liability. All the persons involved in the incident should participate. Administration must provide a *safe* environment for open discussions if the process is to be productive.

Q

QUESTIONS

List four procedures that should be included in an effective suicide prevention plan.

- _____
- _____
- _____
- _____

(4)

When a suicide occurs, your facility's administrators should conduct an _____ of the events surrounding the tragedy.

(11)

Suicide Litigation: Case Law Review

In a landmark case, the U.S. Supreme Court (the highest court in the United States) made the following key statements:

"The government [has an] obligation to provide medical care for [offenders] . . . It is but just that the public be required to care for [offenders], who cannot, by reason of the deprivation of [their] liberty, care for [themselves].

"We . . . conclude that deliberate indifference to serious medical needs of [offenders] constitutes the 'unnecessary and wanton infliction of pain' [prohibited] by the Eighth Amendment [of the U.S. Constitution]. This is true whether the indifference is manifested by [facility] doctors or by [correctional officers/juvenile caseworkers] intentionally denying or delaying access to medical care or intentionally interfering with the treatment once [it's] prescribed.

"[An offender] must allege acts or omissions sufficiently harmful to [show] deliberate indifference to serious medical needs. It is only such indifference that can offend 'evolving standards of decency' in violation of the Eighth Amendment.

"[Offenders] with suicidal tendencies have . . . problems which constitute a 'serious medical need' to which . . . correctional officers [and juvenile caseworkers] cannot be deliberately indifferent." [*Estelle vs. Gamble*, 429 U.S. 97 (1976)]

The important message from these statements is that you must look for signs and symptoms of suicidal behavior among the offenders you supervise. If you notice an offender who is at risk, you must take the appropriate action. Failure to do so could lead to liability.

Listed below are representative case summaries of suicide-related lawsuits. They are good examples of what can happen when correctional staff fail to carry out their duty of care, or worse yet, commit shocking, reckless acts. (This listing is not intended to be all inclusive.)

Hare vs. City of Corinth

Tina Hare was arrested for petty larceny and forgery, and incarcerated in the city jail. During interrogation, police learned that she was addicted to dilaudid, a painkiller; displayed signs of withdrawal; and appeared depressed over her arrest and fitness as a mother. Hare told the investigating officer that she would kill herself if she was put in a cell. He did not take her threat seriously but instructed a police dispatcher to keep an eye on her. In turn, an inmate trustee was told to check on Hare every 45 minutes. The trustee later found Hare hanging from the bars in her cell by a noose fashioned from strips of a blanket. Because she did not have access to the cell, the trustee notified the dispatcher. According to the jail's procedures, the dispatcher could not leave his post. Therefore, he called the investigating officer at home and, shockingly, was instructed to **leave the offender hanging** until the state investigator arrived.

An appeals court said, "In the case . . . there is both the placing of Tina Hare in an isolated cell in her allegedly unstable and agitated condition, and the failure to respond immediately when she was discovered hanging. If the facts alleged by Hare's family are proven, a jury is entitled to find that the actions taken by [the staff], both commission and omission, equal or exceed deliberate indifference to serious medical needs." The case has been sent back to the trial court; a decision is still pending. [*Hare v. City of Corinth (MS)*, 22 F.3rd 612 (5th Cir. 1994)]

Simmons vs. City of Philadelphia

Daniel Simmons was arrested for public intoxication and transported to a police precinct lockup for "protective custody." The arresting officer told the booking officer that Simmons appeared to be heavily intoxicated and was agitated and crying. During the first few hours of incarceration, the booking officer saw that Simmons "had glassy eyes . . . was in a stupor" and his behavior ranged from confusion to hysteria. The booking officer subsequently discovered Daniel Simmons hanging from the bars in the cell by his trousers. Correctional officers cut Simmons down and called paramedics. But the booking officer did not initiate any life-saving measures. Simmons's family filed suit alleging that the city violated Simmons's constitutional right "through a policy or custom of inattention amounting to deliberate indifference to the serious medical needs of intoxicated and potentially suicidal detainees." At trial, the family attorney presented evidence that showed for a five year period, the city's police department experienced 20 suicides in its lockups, did not provide suicide prevention training to its officers, did not assess the suicide risk of offenders at intake, and did not take any other suicide prevention measures. An expert testified that trained officers would have recognized the suicide danger signs and known that Simmons was a high risk for suicidal behavior.

The appeals court stated that "the evidence of 20 jail suicides in the Philadelphia prison system between 1980–85, of whom 15 were intoxicated, the City's possession of knowledge before 1981 that intoxicated detainees presented a high risk of suicide, its awareness of published standards for suicide prevention, and its failure to implement the recommendations of experts, including its own director of mental health services for the prison system, was sufficient basis for the jury to have found that the unnamed officials with responsibility over the City's prisons acted recklessly or with deliberate indifference, thereby contributing to the deprivation of constitutional rights of [Simmons]. If a city cannot be held liable when its policy makers had notice of a problem and failed to act, then it is difficult to posit a set of facts on which a city could be held liable to have been deliberately indifferent." Simmons's family was awarded over $1,104,000. The appeals court rejected the city's argument that only .00015 percent of its offender population committed suicide, stating, "Individual probabilities are a misleading measure of the totality of the constitutional injury suffered by the particular group."

Ironically, the City of Philadelphia later trained all of its officers in suicide prevention at a cost of only $4,000. Since then, there has been a 70 percent reduction in completed suicides. [*Simmons v. City of Philadelphia*, 947 F.2nd 1042 (3rd Cir. 1991)]

Buffington vs. Baltimore County

Buffington's family called police and said that he had left home with several rifles and handguns. Buffington left a suicide note that was given to police. Buffington, with a long history of depression and substance abuse, was arrested and placed under protective custody At booking, an officer asked Buffington what he was going to do with all those guns, to which he replied—"I was going to shoot myself." As per departmental policy, the arresting officers handcuffed Buffington to the bar at the booking desk for processing. The arresting officers then began doing the necessary paperwork to commit Buffington to a psychiatric hospital on an emergency basis. Soon thereafter, a cellblock officer placed Buffington in a cellblock isolation cell, contrary to "unwritten" policy. Within one hour, Buffington was found hanging from the bars in the cell by his trousers. Correctional officers immediately cut him down and initiated CPR, but he later died at the hospital.

The court stated, "This particular injury would have been avoided by the individual desk officers taking the minimal preventive step of following the precinct's official policy and customary practice of keeping Buffington handcuffed to the rail. . . ." The family was awarded $185,000. [*Buffington v. Baltimore County*, 913 F.2nd 113 (4th Cir. 1990)]

Garcia vs. El Paso County

Vincent Garcia was arrested for several motor vehicle violations, including suspicion of drunk driving, and transported to the El Paso County Jail. He expressed fear of being housed in the general population and was placed in a second floor isolation cell. Approximately six hours later, Garcia was found hanging from the bars in his cell by a blanket. It marked the third suicide at the facility in less than 12 months. The family filed a lawsuit and was awarded $10,000. The county agreed to:

- Provide intensive supervision of all recently admitted offenders during the first 24 hours.

- Replace the solid steel doors on all of the existing holding cells in the booking area with "Lexan" glass doors, or similar material.

- Modify the existing light fixtures, ventilator covers, and other protrusions in all holding cells as recommended by an expert in jail architecture.

- Create and maintain a special ward for mental health purposes in which anyone who is in need of special observation as identified by a doctor, psychologist, licensed mental health professional, or jail personnel will be confined.

- Provide intensive and recurring training in suicide prevention, crisis intervention and mental health to all booking, intake, and emergency medical technicians employed by the jail.

Suicide Litigation: Case Law Review (continued)

- Provide intensive screening for risk of suicide to all inmates at the time of booking, using an in-depth questionnaire.

- Contract for the services of an appropriately licensed mental health professional to be on call 24 hours a day to assist jail personnel involved in the booking/screening/classifying roles to identify individuals who require intensive supervision and who have other mental health needs.

- Close Cells 212 and 312 (isolation cells) in a manner that will prevent any use of these cells for confinement of offenders.

- It is contemplated that a new jail will be constructed in El Paso County, pursuant to the American Correctional Association's (ACA) standards. The facility, once constructed, will make reasonable good-faith efforts to seek ACA accreditation. *Note:* The new jail was occupied in 1988 and accredited in 1991.

- Defendants agree that a copy of this Consent Decree will be furnished to all employees of the El Paso County Jail.

This case is a typical example of the *systemic* changes that result from most suicide-related lawsuits. [*Garcia v. Board of County Commissioners of the County of El Paso*, C.A. 83-Z-222 (D.CO.1985)]

Myers vs. Lake County

In one case, the court found that there was no deliberate indifference but the county was negligent. This basically means that staff did something that reasonable people wouldn't have done. Or, the staff failed to do something that reasonable people would do. In other words, the staff did not carry out their duties to protect the offender against unreasonable risk of harm. The jury found the county negligent in preventing a juvenile's suicide attempt in the Lake County Juvenile Detention Center. The 16-year-old suffered permanent brain damage in the attempt. The U.S. District Court awarded $600,000 to the juvenile. Applying Indiana law, the jury found the facility negligent because it did not take adequate precautions against suicide attempts. The appeals court upheld the ruling and the award. The court decided that the law required the facility to use reasonable care to prevent juveniles from attempting suicide. [*Myers v. County of Lake, IN*, 30F.3d 847 (7th Cir. 1994), *Cert. denied*, 115 S. Ct. 666]

Summary

This chapter identified ways you can avoid liability in suicide-related lawsuits, and examined the key parts of an effective suicide prevention plan.

1. Identify four ways correctional staff can avoid liability in suicide-related lawsuits.

   - Correctional workers can avoid liability in suicide-related lawsuits by following established policies, procedures, job descriptions, and professional training.

   - The "we-minded" team worker usually adheres to such practices. This type of individual has learned to control his or her negative attitudes, biases, and prejudices.

2. Describe at least six parts of an effective suicide prevention plan.

   - One of the best ways to avoid liability is by following the procedures in your facility's suicide prevention plan.

   - An effective plan includes procedures for:

     — *Identifying* newly admitted offenders who are potentially suicidal

     — *Training* all staff to detect and prevent suicides

     — *Assessing* potentially suicidal offenders

     — *Monitoring* or supervising potentially suicidal offenders

     — *Housing* potentially suicidal offenders properly

     — *Referring* potentially suicidal offenders to mental health services

     — *Communicating* to other staff—including mental health staff—about potentially suicidal offenders

     — *Intervening* to prevent suicides

     — *Notifying* officials, family members, and significant others about attempted or completed suicides

     — *Reporting* and documenting attempted or completed suicides

     — *Participating* in the "**administrative review**" where the administration provides a safe environment for open and frank discussions about attempted and completed suicides

3. Identify two guidelines for properly housing suicidal offenders.

   - You must constantly supervise a suicidal offender who is placed in isolation. If this is not possible, the offender should be placed with "companions." In this situation, you must supervise the offender at least every ten minutes.

   - If you place potentially suicidal offenders in suicide-resistant rooms, you need to supervise them every **three to four minutes** because some offenders do commit suicide in these settings by very "creative" techniques. It takes less than ten minutes for a successful suicide to occur.

Note: Two-thirds of all suicides in custody occur in isolation.

1. To avoid liability, correctional workers must follow established:

   - Policies

   - Procedures

   - Job descriptions

   - Professional training

2. You should not place potentially suicidal offenders in isolation unless they can be **constantly** supervised—observed.

3. You can prevent a suicide attempt or death by:

   - Listening

   - Questioning

   - Referring offenders to mental health services

   - Providing immediate first aid when needed

4. Effective suicide prevention plans should include procedures for: (choose four)

   - Identification

   - Training

   - Assessment

   - Monitoring

   - Housing

   - Referral

   - Communication

   - Intervention

   - Notification

   - Reporting

   - Administrative review

Answer Key—Avoiding Liability in Suicide-Related Lawsuits (continued)

5. The most likely to be held liable in a lawsuit is:

    __✓__ A. "I-me" worker

    _____ B. "We-minded" worker

    _____ C. Team worker

    _____ D. Both B and C

6. **False**. In this situation, you must still supervise potentially suicidal offenders—**at least every ten minutes**.

7. **False**. The "duty to warn" principle requires that mental health professionals relay their opinions of suicide potential to correctional workers. This practice does not violate the offender's confidentiality in relation to mental health records.

8. **True**. A good way to avoid liability is to follow your facility's suicide prevention plan.

9. If a potentially suicidal offender is in a suicide-resistant room, you must supervise him every **three** to **four** minutes.

10. **False**. Correctional workers, as well as medical staff, should know how to respond to a suicide attempt.

11. When a suicide occurs, your facility's administrators should conduct an "**administrative review**" of the events surrounding the tragedy.

12. **True**. Clues or signs of potentially suicidal behavior can be verbal or non-verbal (behavioral).

The Impact of Facility Design on Offender Management and Suicide Prevention

Objectives

At the end of this chapter, participants will be able to:

1. Cite American Correctional Association standards about the location of correctional worker posts and staff training for responding to suicide attempts and other emergencies.

2. Describe at least ten aspects of custodial architecture/design that help to make a facility suicide resistant.

Introduction

Although the most important suicide prevention factor is a sufficient number of trained staff, proper design of cells/rooms is also important. Living areas should be designed so that:

• They are suicide resistant

• They aid in supervising or monitoring potentially suicidal offenders

For example, direct supervision or new generations jails by their very design provide a much *safer* environment than linear/older jails—for not only preventing suicides but also for reducing offender assaults and same-sex rapes. There are officer posts *inside* the pods or modules. Thus, the officers know their offenders much better and are able to note *behavior changes* more readily.

CAUTION: Two-thirds of suicides in custody occur in *single* rooms/cells. Even if your facility has suicide-resistant living quarters, experts recommend that staff directly supervise suicidal offenders.

You are not responsible for the design of your facility and ensuring that it has suicide-resistant features. However, you should be familiar with such features so that you can help to provide a safe environment for suicidal offenders. For example, suppose you must place an offender in an area that is not "suicide-resistant." You will have a better awareness of what items pose a danger and can make suggestions to your supervisor for future renovations. Likewise, if the room is suicide-resistant and an item is broken, you can inform your supervisor about the potential hazard.

This chapter will highlight those factors essential to making living areas suicide-resistant in new and remodeled facilities.

Facility Design

The American Correctional Association's standards recommend that correctional workers be stationed inside or immediately adjacent to offender housing areas. The standards also require correctional workers to respond to emergencies within four minutes, which may save a hanging victim. When they do not meet these standards, facilities increase the risk of completed suicides.

Unfortunately, facilities seldom have enough staff to provide constant supervision of suicidal people. That is why good facility design and layout are so important. They can greatly aid in monitoring or supervising potentially suicidal offenders by providing protrusion-free cells/rooms and avoiding blind spots that cannot be easily monitored.

Q QUESTIONS

American Correctional Association standards require correctional workers to respond to emergencies within:

_____ A. Two minutes

_____ B. Fifteen minutes

_____ C. Four minutes

_____ D. Ten minutes

(3)

American Correctional Association standards recommend that correctional worker posts be located:

_____ A. Within 30 feet of the living areas

_____ B. At strategic points

_____ C. Inside or immediately adjacent to living areas

_____ D. Within 50 feet of housing areas

(11)

Protrusion-Free Architecture

As a correctional worker, you are not responsible for the design of your facility. However, you should be aware of how to make living areas suicide-resistant—so that you can spot potential problems or hazards and report them to your supervisor.

In general, all easy-access protrusions (projections, extensions) should be removed from cells and sleeping rooms. At a minimum, they should be removed from suicide/mental health, segregation, and holding cells.

Other items should be modified or altered to make them suicide-resistant. Bars and air grilles are the most common fixtures used for attaching suicide nooses. But shelves, beds, benches, sprinklers, towel racks, door handles, floor drain covers, and plumbing fixtures also might be used in a suicide attempt as well.

CAUTION: Offenders have committed suicide in "suicide-resistant" rooms/cells by stuffing toilet paper or clothing in their nostrils and mouth, thus closing off their oxygen supply. You must be vigilant when supervising offenders in these rooms/cells.

Below are some good techniques for making items in living areas/cells/rooms suicide-resistant:

- Cover bars with one-fourth-inch polycarbonate glazing (clear plastic, scratch-resistant sheeting or glass substitute) or heavy detention/security screen, with openings no greater than one-eighth inch.

You should be aware of how to make living areas suicide-resistant—so that you can spot potential problems or hazards and report them to your supervisor.

QUESTIONS

Offenders commonly attach nooses to:

_____ A. Beds

_____ B. Bars and air grilles

_____ C. Plumbing fixtures

_____ D. Door hinges

(9)

To be suicide-resistant, air grilles should have openings no greater than _____ inch.

(1)

True/False   Staff can relax and not worry about offenders committing suicide in suicide-resistant cells or rooms.

(12)

CHAPTER 11
The Impact of Facility Design on Offender
Management and Suicide Prevention

Protrusion-Free Architecture (continued)

- Add a security screen to vents, grilles, ducts, and light fixtures by spot-welding or using non-removable screws. The opening should be no more than one-eighth inch in diameter.

- Replace solid fixtures or so-called collapsible clothes hooks (which can be jammed with any small object, such as a pencil, a plastic spoon handle, a twig, or a small stone) with ball-in-socket, non-blockable types.

- Remove small door panels and a portion of solid front walls (to create windows), and replace with polycarbonate glazing.

- Repair or replace typical steel beds. This way, offenders cannot commit suicide **under** them. Offenders can attach a noose overhead, run it under their necks and turn over on their stomachs. In about 15–30 seconds, they lose consciousness. In about 12–13 minutes, with their oxygen cut off, they suffocate. Only the weight of the head is needed to stop the flow of oxygen and blood. If possible, install solid concrete slab beds with rounded edges or totally enclosed heavy molded plastic.

QUESTIONS

True/False   Security screens should be added to vents, grilles, ducts, and light fixtures to make them suicide-resistant.

(8)

True/False   Offenders cannot commit suicide under steel beds—there's no room to do it.

(4)

Protrusion-Free Architecture (continued)

- Paint cells and sleeping rooms in pastel colors. Also, paint headers above cell doors black or another dark color to reduce camera glare and create contrast. These techniques make closed circuit television monitoring (CCTV) more effective for suicide prevention.

- Install an audio-monitoring intercom in cells/rooms to help detect suicide attempts and other emergencies. For example, hangings often produce noise such as gurgling and thrashing sounds.

- Locate the suicide observation room near the nursing or control station for good audio and visual monitoring.

- Provide modesty shields or screens with triangular, rounded, or sloping tops. The shields or screens should have no surface where a noose could be anchored. Make sure that an offender's feet can be observed when he or she is behind the shield or screen.

Q

QUESTIONS

What can be done to make closed circuit television monitoring (CCTV) more effective for suicide prevention?

- _____
- _____

(2)

The suicide observation room should be near the _____ station.

(7)

Protrusion-Free Architecture (continued)

- Install solid, triangular end plates to shelf tops and exposed hinges. This way, a noose cannot be attached to them.

- Use only fire-retardant mattresses that do not produce toxic fumes.

- Anchor desk tops to the wall with solid triangular end plates. Once again, a noose cannot be attached to this type of plate.

- Remove any metal, plastic, or glass from cells/rooms that can be used as a cutting tool.

Q QUESTIONS

Nooses cannot be attached to _____ end plates.
(10)

Fire-retardant mattresses should be used because they do not produce _____ fumes.
(5)

Protrusion-Free Architecture (continued)

- Light high-risk suicide units sufficiently for 24-hour CCTV surveillance. Infrared filters over the ceiling lights produce total darkness but CCTV picks up images as if it were daylight. Lighting during the daytime would need to be provided separately.

- Install sprinklers flush with the ceiling. Use breakaway sprinklers. These sprinklers drop down or protrude when set off. Or, place protective cones on exposed sprinklers. These cones cover the sprinklers except for one-third inch of the tips. This way, offenders cannot hang themselves on exposed sprinklers.

- Make sure that floor drain openings are no more than one-eighth inch in diameter.

Many "safe" cells/rooms, including padded cells, have floor drains with openings larger than one-eighth inch. The offender may use the hem of his undershirt or shorts to make a noose. He affixes a slip knot to his neck and places the "rope" over his shoulder. Then, in a kneeling position, he attaches the end of the "rope" to the floor drain. By leaning into it, the noose tightens and within a maximum of 30 seconds, he will pass out. Within 12–13 minutes total asphyxiation will occur. A one-

eighth inch opening will prevent the offender from tying the "rope" to the drain. If you see a floor drain in a padded cell—or any other type of suicide watch room—that has too large an opening, alert your maintenance supervisor to the problem. Retrofitting can correct the problem.

Some "safe" cells/rooms have cross bars and/or other configurations to which a noose can be attached.

QUESTIONS

How can your facility prevent offenders from hanging themselves on exposed sprinklers?

- _____

- _____

(6)

Summary

This chapter highlighted those factors essential to making living areas suicide-resistant in new and remodeled facilities.

1. Cite American Correctional Association standards about the location of correctional worker posts and staff training for responding to suicide attempts and other emergencies.

   • The standards recommend that correctional workers be stationed inside or immediately adjacent to offender housing areas.

   • The standards also recommend that correctional workers respond to emergencies within four minutes.

2. Describe at least ten aspects of custodial architecture/design that help to make a facility suicide resistant.

   • Good facility design and layout can greatly aid in monitoring or supervising potentially suicidal offenders by providing protrusion-free cells/rooms and avoiding blind spots that cannot be easily monitored.

   • As a correctional worker, you are not responsible for the design of your facility. However, you should be aware of how to make living areas suicide-resistant—so that you can spot potential problems or hazards and report them to your supervisor.

   • In general, all easy-access protrusions (projections, extensions) should be removed from cells and sleeping rooms. At a minimum, they should be removed from suicide/mental health, segregation, and holding cells.

   • Other items should be modified or altered to make them suicide-resistant— bars and air grilles, shelves, beds, benches, sprinklers, towel racks, door handles, and plumbing fixtures.

   • CAUTION: Two-thirds of suicides in custody occur in *single* rooms and cells. "Imaginative" suicides have even occurred in suicide-resistant quarters. Maximum supervision, often-times constant or continuous, is required for high-risk offenders.

   • Add a security screen to vents, grilles, ducts, and light fixtures.

   • Replace solid fixtures or so-called collapsible clothes hooks with ball-in-socket, non-blockable types.

   • Remove a portion of solid front walls (to create windows), and replace with polycarbonate glazing.

   • Repair or replace typical steel beds, closing off the area below each bed.

- Paint cells and sleeping rooms in pastel colors. Also, paint headers above cell doors black or another dark color to reduce camera glare and create contrast.

- Install an audio-monitoring intercom in cells/rooms to listen for gurgling, thrashing, and other sounds produced by hangings.

- Locate the suicide observation room near the nursing or control station.

- Provide modesty shields or screens with triangular, rounded, or sloping tops. The shields or screens should have no surface where a noose could be anchored. Make sure that an offender's feet can be observed when he or she is behind the shield or screen.

- Install solid, triangular end plates to shelf tops and exposed hinges.

- Use only fire-retardant mattresses that do not produce toxic fumes.

- Anchor desk tops to the wall with solid triangular end plates.

- Remove from cells/rooms any metal, plastic, or glass that can be used as a cutting tool.

- Light high-risk suicide units sufficiently for 24-hour CCTV surveillance.

- Install sprinklers flush with the ceiling. Use breakaway sprinklers, or place protective cones on exposed sprinklers.

- Make sure that floor drain openings are no more than one-eighth inch in diameter.

Answer Key—The Impact of Facility Design on Offender Management and Suicide Prevention

1. To be suicide-resistant, air grilles should have openings no greater than **one-eighth** inch.

2. To make closed circuit television monitoring (CCTV) more effective for suicide prevention, your facility can:

    - Paint cells and sleeping rooms in pastel colors

    - Paint headers above cell doors black or another dark color

3. American Correctional Association standards require correctional workers to respond to emergencies within:

    _____ A. Two minutes

    _____ B. Fifteen minutes

    ✓ C. Four minutes

    _____ D. Ten minutes

4. **False**. Offenders **can** commit suicide under steel beds. Offenders can attach a noose overhead, run it under their necks and turn over on their stomachs. In about 15–30 seconds, they lose consciousness. In about 12–13 minutes, with their oxygen cut off, they suffocate.

5. Fire-retardant mattresses should be used because they do not produce **toxic** fumes.

6. Your facility can prevent offenders from hanging themselves on exposed sprinklers by:

    - Using breakaway sprinklers, or

    - Placing protective cones on exposed sprinklers

7. The suicide observation room should be near the **nursing or control** station.

8. **True**. Security screens should be added to vents, grilles, ducts, and light fixtures to make them suicide-resistant.

9. Offenders commonly attach nooses to:

    _____ A. Beds

    ✓ B. Bars and air grilles

    _____ C. Plumbing fixtures

    _____ D. Door hinges

10. Nooses cannot be attached to **solid, triangular** end plates.

Answer Key—The Impact of Facility Design on Offender Management and Suicide Prevention (continued)

11. American Correctional Association standards recommend that correctional worker posts be located:

    _____ A. Within 30 feet of the living areas

    _____ B. At strategic points

    __✓__ C. Inside or immediately adjacent to living areas

    _____ D. Within 50 feet of housing areas

12. **False.** Offenders have used imaginative methods of killing themselves, even in "suicide-resistant" cells/rooms. Vigilance must exist, not complacency.

143

CHAPTER TWELVE

Responding to the Suicide Victim

Objectives

At the end of this chapter, you will be able to:

1. Identify at least two items that should be available in housing units to help you rescue a suicide victim.

2. Identify the seven steps for responding to a hanging victim.

3. Identify the five steps for responding to self-harm victims.

4. List four precautions you can take to keep from contracting an infectious disease in response to a suicide attempt.

Introduction

Some offenders die in their suicide attempts because correctional workers do not perform first aid. Sometimes, correctional workers look for vital signs, find none, and assume that the victim is dead.

Only a physician or other qualified* health professional(s), as designated by state law, can pronounce a person dead. Until the victim is pronounced dead, or qualified health personnel can take over, you should start and continue first aid and cardiopulmonary resuscitation (CPR). Many "dead people" are alive today because someone followed this principle.

This chapter will discuss recognized practices and procedures for giving first aid to hanging and other deliberate self-harm victims.

Qualified health personnel are licensed, registered, and certified.

Emergency Rescue Equipment

Offenders usually commit suicide when they are alone in their cells/rooms. To rescue offenders, you must respond immediately. You will not have time to wait for medical help or receive instructions about what to do. Similarly, you must have the equipment you need "at your fingertips." You will not have time to radio for tools or other items. Each housing unit or living area, therefore, should have the following equipment, at a minimum.

- First aid kit
- Emergency rescue cutting tool
- CPR face mask
- Latex gloves

CAUTION: Some correctional workers fail to revive victims because they spend too much time trying to locate a cutting tool. Some facilities require officers to carry or have readily available the "911 Rescue Tool," or seat-belt cutter. This tool is available at or through most police uniform and supply stores. Facilities using it verify the manufacturer's claim: "Will not slash or stab—cannot be used as a life-threatening weapon."

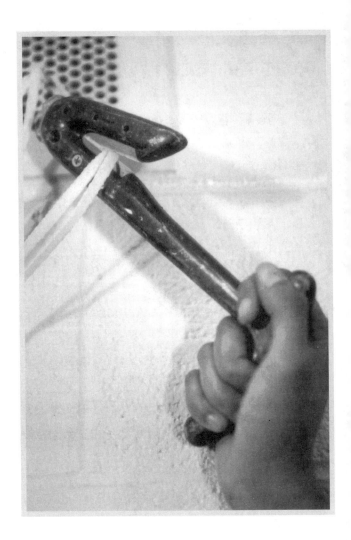

The overwhelming majority of suicides in custody are hangings. A hanging attempt may affect all of the neck structures: the airway, spinal cord, and major blood vessels. When you come upon a hanging victim, therefore, be sure to:

1. Cut the victim down rapidly, protecting his or her head and neck. One person should hold the victim up while another cuts, loosens, or removes the noose.

Remember that brain damage can occur in four minutes and death in five or six minutes from the start of a hanging. A delay on your part of one or two minutes could cause brain damage or death. In addition, if you fail to respond promptly to a hanging victim, you and your facility can be held liable in a lawsuit. In one case, for example, the court ruled that:

"There was clear evidence from which a jury could find that Heflin died as a proximate cause of the failure of Sheriff Hicks and Deputy Crutcher to take steps to save his life. They left Heflin hanging for twenty minutes or more after discovering him. . . . The jailer should have cut the victim down immediately with one person holding the body up and the other cutting the noose. Officers should never stand by and let the hanging victim continue to hang in order to protect the 'scene of the crime.' Further, even though there were no vital signs, officers should never presume that death has already occurred. 'Dead' people are alive today due to CPR. On the contrary, officers should presume that the hanging inmate is alive and administer first aid until told by a physician to stop." [*Heflin v. Stewart County*, 958 F. 2nd 709 (6th cur. 1992)]

QUESTIONS

Brain damage can occur in _____ minutes and death in _____ or _____ from the start of a hanging.

(1)

When you're cutting down a hanging victim, you should protect his or her _____ and _____ .

(3)

Only a _____ or other qualified _____, as designated by state law, can pronounce a person dead.

(5)

True/False   If a hanging victim has no vital signs, you should assume he or she is dead and take no further action.

(7)

Responding to the Hanging Victim (continued)

2. Call an ambulance and in-house health care personnel immediately.

Procedures for handling an emergency may vary in each facility. When a suicide attempt occurs, you should follow your facility's policies and procedures for notifying the appropriate officials. If your facility has a policy that states, "Notify your supervisor first in case of a suicide," discuss with your supervisor what you should do when he or she is not nearby. Specifically, ask your supervisor how much discretion you have in dealing with life-safety matters.

Remember, you must respond quickly to the victim. Thus, you may need another staff member to make the necessary calls while you and another officer tend to the victim.

True/False   Before a suicide attempt occurs, you should discuss with your supervisor how much discretion you have in dealing with life-safety matters.

QUESTIONS

(17)

First Aid for Hanging Victims

As a correctional worker, you should have received training in first aid. You also should receive refresher training every other year to keep your skills sharp and up-to-date. To review, the basic techniques for administering first aid to a hanging victim are:

1. Monitor and maintain the victim's airway.

- Look, listen, and feel for breathing, if he is unconscious.

- Maintain the airway, if necessary, using the *modified jaw thrust*. DO NOT tilt the victim's head back because you may injure his spinal cord.

  —Place your fingers behind the angles of the lower jaw.

  —Forcefully bring the jaw forward.

  —Use your thumbs to pull the lower lip down, to allow breathing through the mouth and nose.

- Give artificial respiration, if necessary, while maintaining the jaw thrust to keep the airway open.

  —Give CPR if there is no pulse.

  —**Assume the spinal cord is injured and treat accordingly, so that you don't cause further injury.**

  - Place the victim flat on the floor *outside* the cell or room with his head held stable. Never place the victim on a bed.

  - Do not let the victim or anyone lift or twist the victim's head.

  - Do not give the victim anything to eat or drink, and do not give him or her any medications.

2. If there is swelling or discoloration, apply an ice bag to the affected area.

3. Do NOT leave the victim alone.

4. Arrange for psychological help when the victim is medically able to receive it.

Q QUESTIONS

True/False   The traditional CPR method of tilting the head back to open the airway is used on hanging victims.

(12)

True/False   When you're giving first aid to a hanging victim, you should assume his or her spinal cord is injured and treat accordingly.

(4)

When the hanging victim is medically able to receive it, you should arrange for _____ help.

(10)

A hanging victim should not be given any _____, drink, or

_____.

(8)

151

First Aid for Deliberate Self-Harm Victims

Deliberate self-harm (DSH) by cutting may be a manipulative or an attention-getting act. However, some manipulative or attention-getters *do* kill themselves by suicide. Unfortunately, experience has shown that some staff lose patience with DSH offenders who repeat their acts. Such staff get tired of responding to those offenders who "take up their time" and "need too much attention." You must be especially careful not to fall into this trap. You must *control* your negative attitudes and comments. Otherwise, your behavior and statements may trigger a retaliatory suicide attempt by an offender that results in death and a lawsuit.

To achieve this control and respond properly to the DSH offender, remember to view each act as a *first* suicide attempt. Administer first aid *immediately*; do not delay treatment.

An individual may go into shock and lose consciousness from losing as little as one quart of blood. **Death from bleeding can occur quickly.**

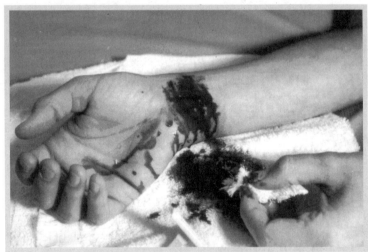

First Aid for Deliberate Self-Harm Victims (continued)

To review, the first aid techniques for bleeding victims are:

1. Control the external bleeding by applying direct pressure to the wound, elevating the injured limb/area, and applying pressure on the artery. (These first aid measures may be done in any order.)

2. Call an ambulance and in-house health care personnel immediately.

Once again, procedures for handling an emergency may vary in each facility. When a suicide attempt occurs, you should follow your facility's policies and procedures for notifying the appropriate officials. You may need another staff member to make the necessary calls while you and another officer tend to the victim—because time is crucial in providing first aid/CPR.

3. Tell the in-house health care personnel or emergency room staff if:

   • The wound looks like it will require stitches

   • The victim has lost a cup or more of blood

4. Do NOT leave the victim alone.

5. Arrange for psychological help when the victim is medically able to receive it.

Q

QUESTIONS

True/False   Death from bleeding occurs slowly.

(2)

True/False   Although deliberate self-harm by cutting may be manipulative or attention-getting behavior, you must treat the act as a first suicide attempt.

(16)

External bleeding is controlled by:

• _____

• _____

• _____

(9)

You should tell in-house health care personnel or emergency room staff if the:

____   A.   Wound looks like it will require stitches

____   B.   Offender has attempted suicide before

____   C.   Family should be notified

____   D.   Victim has lost a cup or more of blood

(11)

The AIDS Scare

AIDS (Acquired Immune Deficiency Syndrome) has drastically changed the way we approach first aid. Since AIDS is a fatal disease, it is the center of many fears and myths. For some correctional workers, the thought of administering first aid or CPR to a victim may provoke a fear of catching AIDS. This thought is perfectly natural. However, *you can protect yourself from getting AIDS or other diseases and still provide the necessary care by using barrier devices.* Here are two precautions for an emergency situation:

- Use a face mask or breather tube when administering CPR. A breather tube will allow you to breathe air into a victim without putting your mouth over his mouth. This practice not only prevents the transmission of the AIDS virus (through blood) but also prevents the transmission of other infectious diseases.

- If no breather tube or face mask is available, place a handkerchief over the victim's mouth and breathe through it.

If a victim's heart and/or breathing have stopped, he is likely to die unless given immediate assistance. Every second you wait reduces the victim's chances for survival. As a correctional worker, you are obligated to perform CPR when an offender or a staff member needs it—even if protective equipment is not available.

Note: There have been no documented cases of a person catching AIDS from another person's saliva.

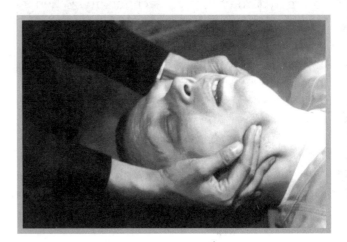

QUESTIONS

Many facilities provide _____ , which allow rescuers to administer CPR without placing their mouths over the mouths of victims.

(13)

True/False   The AIDS virus is not transmitted through saliva.

(6)

If face masks or breather tubes are not available, you should:

____ A. Not perform CPR

____ B. Place a handkerchief over the victim's mouth and breathe through it

____ C. Call a supervisor to ask advice

____ D. See what your facility's policies and procedures manual says to do

(15)

Cleaning Up Blood and Other Body Fluids

After an emergency is over, you may be involved with cleaning up blood and other body fluids. Cleaning up these kinds of fluids used to be a routine task. Since the discovery of the AIDS virus, however, this task has become a serious matter; it requires several precautions on your part:

- Be *careful* if you have cuts, scratches, or open wounds on your hands. Even if your hands are "clear" (no cuts), wear disposable rubber or plastic gloves to avoid contacting potentially tainted blood or other body fluids.

- Clean up any surface contaminated with blood or body fluids with a mixture of household bleach and water—approximately 1/4 cup of bleach to one gallon of water. Other disinfectants, such as alcohol, Lysol, or industrial strength cleaners, are also effective in killing the AIDS virus. Be sure to wear your gloves.

- Wash your hands and arms *carefully*. If you come into contact with any blood or body fluid, wash immediately.

- Dispose of gloves and soiled sponges or towels properly.

The federal Occupational Safety and Health Administration (OSHA) requires your facility to provide training in this area. If you have not received this training, talk with your supervisor.

OSHA recommends that you also:

- Carry a pouch with two pairs of gloves

- Follow universal precautions: treat any blood or body fluid as if it were infected

Q

QUESTIONS

If you have to clean up blood or other body fluids, you should:

- _____
- _____
- _____
- _____
- _____
- _____

(14)

Summary

This chapter outlined recognized practices and procedures for giving first aid to hanging and deliberate self-harm/cutting victims.

1. Identify at least two items that should be available in housing units to help you rescue a suicide victim.

   - First aid kit

   - Emergency rescue cutting tool

   - CPR face mask

   - Latex gloves

2. Identify the seven steps for responding to a hanging victim.

   - Cut the victim down rapidly, protecting his head and neck. One person should hold the victim up while another cuts, loosens, or removes the noose.

   - Call an ambulance and in-house health care personnel immediately.

   - Administer first aid:

     — Monitor and maintain the victim's airway.

     — If there is swelling or discoloration, apply an ice bag to the affected area.

     — Do NOT leave the victim alone.

     — Arrange for psychological help when the victim is medically able to receive it.

3. Identify the five steps for responding to self-harm victims.

   - Control external bleeding by applying direct pressure to the wound, elevating the injured area, and applying pressure on the artery.

   - Call an ambulance and in-house health care personnel immediately.

   - Tell the in-house health care personnel or emergency room staff if:

     — The wound looks like it will require stitches

     — The victim has lost a cup or more of blood

   - Do NOT leave the victim alone.

   - Arrange for psychological help when the victim is medically able to receive it.

4. List four precautions you can take to keep from contracting an infectious disease in response to a suicide attempt.

   - Use a face mask or breather tube when administering CPR. If no breather tube or face mask is available, place a handkerchief over the victim's mouth and breathe through it.

   - Be *careful* if you have cuts, scratches, or open wounds on your hands. Even if your hands are not cut, wear disposable rubber or plastic gloves to avoid contacting potentially tainted blood or other body fluids.

   - Clean up any surface contaminated with blood or body fluids with a mixture of household bleach and water—approximately 1/4 cup of bleach to one gallon of water. Other disinfectants, such as alcohol, Lysol, or industrial strength cleaners, are also effective in killing the AIDS virus. Be sure to wear your gloves.

   - Wash your hands and arms *carefully*. If you come into contact with any blood or body fluid, wash immediately.

   - Dispose of gloves and soiled sponges or towels properly.

   - Carry a pouch with two pairs of gloves.

   - Follow universal precautions: treat any blood or body fluid as if it were infected.

Answer Key—Responding to the Suicide Victim

1. Brain damage can occur in **four** minutes and death in **five** or **six** minutes from the start of a hanging.

2. **False**. Death from bleeding occurs *quickly*.

3. When you're cutting down a hanging victim, you should protect his or **head** and **neck.**

4. **True**. When you're giving first aid to a hanging victim, you should assume his or her spinal cord is injured and treat accordingly.

5. Only a **physician** or other qualified **health professional(s)**, as designated by state law, can pronounce a person dead.

6. **True**. The AIDS virus is not transmitted through saliva. It is transmitted through blood or body fluids.

7. **False**. If a hanging victim has no vital signs, you should start first aid/CPR *immediately.*

8. A hanging victim should *not* be given any **food**, drink or **medicine**.

9. External bleeding is controlled by:
   - Direct pressure to the wound
   - Elevation of injured area
   - Pressure on the artery

10. When the hanging victim is medically able to receive it, you should arrange for **psychological** help.

11. You should tell in-house health care personnel or emergency room staff if the:

    _✓_ A. Wound looks like it will require stitches

    _____ B. Offender has attempted suicide before

    _____ C. Family should be notified

    _✓_ D. Victim has lost a cup or more of blood

12. **False**. The *modified jaw thrust* is used to open the airway of a hanging victim.

13. Many facilities provide **face masks or breather tubes**, which allow rescuers to administer CPR without placing their mouths over the mouths of victims.

Answer Key—Responding to the Suicide Victim (continued)

14. If you have to clean up blood or other body fluids, you should:

    - Be *careful* if you have cuts, scratches, or open wounds on your hands. Even if your hands are "clear," wear rubber or plastic gloves

    - Use a solution of bleach and water to clean the spill

    - Wash your hands and arms *carefully*

    - Dispose of gloves and soiled sponges or towels properly

    - Carry a pouch with two pairs of gloves

    - Treat any blood or body fluid as if it were infected

15. If face masks or breather tubes are not available, you should:

    _____ A. Not perform CPR

    _✓_ B. Place a handkerchief over the victim's mouth and breathe through it

    _____ C. Call a supervisor to ask advice

    _____ D. See what your facility's policies and procedures manual says to do

16. **True**. Although deliberate self-harm by cutting may be a manipulative or attention-getting act, you must treat the act as the first suicide attempt—because some manipulators or attention-getters do kill themselves.

17. **True**. Before a suicide attempt occurs, you should discuss with your supervisor how much discretion you have in dealing with life-safety matters. Make sure that you understand your facility's policies and procedures.

CHAPTER THIRTEEN

Administrative Review and Follow-up Support for Staff

Objectives

At the end of this chapter, you will be able to:

1. List at least three issues that are discussed in the administrative review.

2. List at least three items that should be included in the report about the administrative review.

3. Identify at least two positive outcomes of an administrative review.

Introduction

After an attempted or completed suicide in custody has occurred, administrators should conduct a review of the events surrounding the tragedy. This practice provides an opportunity to discuss what might have been done differently, and determine how to prevent another suicide from occurring.

In future lawsuits, courts, juries, and opposing attorneys will consider failure to do this follow-up process as *deliberate indifference*. Moreover, nonresponsiveness to life safety will be considered deliberate indifference as well. For example, if your facility does not correct known life-safety deficiencies and another death occurs, it is nonresponsive to life-safety issues.

This chapter will examine the administrative review. It also will explain the importance of dealing openly with staff feelings about the suicide.

The Administrative Review

Administration and all involved staff should conduct a thorough evaluation of the facts and circumstances surrounding a completed (or an attempted) suicide. This evaluation should be held in addition to the "official" investigation. However, the "administrative review" should also include the official facts and/or report.

The goal of the investigation is to determine criminal liability. In contrast, the goal of the administrative review is to avoid civil liability (a lawsuit against the facility and staff).

Even if your facility does not follow the practice of conducting an administrative review, you should be aware of it—so that you can talk with your supervisor about the possibility of implementing the practice at your facility.

Everyone involved in a suicide (or attempted suicide) should participate in the administrative review and discuss:

Missed Signs and Symptoms: There may have been signs and/or symptoms that were overlooked but, in hindsight, can help prevent future attempts and completed suicides. This part of the review is essential to the training and learning process.

Policies and Procedures: Were there any deficiencies here? Modifications resulting from the review should be incorporated into an updated suicide prevention plan.

Training: Were staff involved in the incident properly trained? Do training and refresher training programs meet recognized practices?

Mental Health and Medical Staff Input: If outside mental health contract staff provided services on the case, they should be included in the administrative review.

Q QUESTIONS

What is an administrative review?

_____

_____

_____

(1)

What is its purpose?

_____

_____

_____

(3)

Staff Concerns: Staff should have an opportunity to express their feelings about the attempted or completed suicide, and facility administrators should *recognize* these feelings. A failure in *communication* is a common problem between health care and correctional personnel in suicide deaths. Most communication failures relate to: 1) Mental health/medical staff failing to alert correctional staff about suicide risk and what level of precaution is needed, and 2) Correctional staff failing to inform mental health/medical staff about new signs/symptoms identified while observing the offender. Open discussion is essential for resolution of this problem. Professional, unemotional "venting" may be all that is necessary to ward off any long-term negative effects.

A productive administrative review will occur only when administration: provides a *safe* environment for staff to openly discuss any shortcomings without any "finger point-ing"; recognizes staff feelings; and fosters open, honest discussion. The agency should encourage and pay for staff referrals (perhaps through an insurance plan) to confidential counseling when needed.

Report: The process should culminate in a written report that identifies the staff in attendance and describes:

- The administrative review (process)
- The circumstances of the incident
- What, if anything, could have been done to prevent the completed suicide from having occurred
- What changes in current policies and procedures, if any, are necessary to reduce the likelihood of such a completed suicide occurring again

The report about the administrative review should be documented and kept on file in case a lawsuit is filed.

QUESTIONS

True/False Correctional workers need to express their feelings about an attempted or completed suicide, and administrators need to recognize those feelings.

(2)

List three things that should be included in the report about the administrative review.

- _____
- _____
- _____

(4)

How can you avoid miscommunication with mental/medical staff about a suicidal offender?

_____

_____

(6)

The Administrative Review (continued)

Suicides can and do occur even when staff have put forth their best effort. Under these circumstances, some correctional workers still blame themselves for "not having done better."

They may suffer from severe guilt feelings that can remain for years. Some might even resign after the suicide because of the way they feel.

Unfortunately, the "we-minded" team worker seems to be the most affected. This worker has a genuine concern for the safety and welfare of both staff and offenders. Thus, an attempted or completed suicide in his or her unit has a tremendous impact. Conversely, the "I-minded" worker, who lacks the concern of the team worker, often is not fazed.

If you find yourself in the midst of guilt over a suicide, remind yourself of this crucial fact: even experienced psychiatrists have admitted that they misjudged suicide victims and, thus, were not able to predict a suicide. There is no shame in seeking help from a counselor.

Q

QUESTIONS

Participants in the administrative review should discuss:

- _____
- _____
- _____
- _____
- _____

(5)

Case Study—Administrative Review

John Rogers was arrested for violating a restraining order and assaulting his wife from whom he was recently separated. She had initiated divorce proceedings two months earlier, contending that his alcohol and drug habits had become more severe. He appeared to be intoxicated at arrest.

During transportation to the Wilson County Jail, Rogers muttered to arresting Officer Huple, "I still love that woman. I don't think I can take it."

At booking, Rogers' response to the health screening question, "Have you ever thought about or attempted to commit suicide?" was, "A couple months ago, I tried to overdose on heroin but found out I didn't have enough of it."

Booking Officer Stanton placed Rogers in a regular single cell. No blood alcohol test was done. Stanton told Rogers that the jail officer would let him make his phone call.

The jail's only cellblock officer, Williams, made regular 30-minute checks, per policy. Before Williams placed Rogers in Cell B-11—farthest from the officer post—Rogers asked to make a phone call . Williams said that the phone call would have to wait until he and the trustee picked up the dinner trays.

About 20 minutes later during rounds, Officer Williams found Rogers hanging by his shirt, attached to the air vent above the sink. His feet were off the floor.

Williams ran to the dispatcher's office, yelled for Mrs. Carroll to call the ambulance, grabbed the cellblock key, and went to booking to get Officer Stanton to help take Rogers down.

Stanton was in the toilet, so there was a delay.

Because neither officer had a knife on their person, Williams ran and grabbed one from the kitchen.

Rogers was cut down and placed on the bed. Williams checked Rogers' vital signs but found none. Williams said to Stanton, "It looks like he's dead." A short time later, the ambulance arrived, and paramedics started CPR and advanced life support measures. The paramedics found a weak pulse, and Rogers was taken to Neal General Hospital. He died within an hour.

State Bureau of Criminal Apprehension Agent Peters interviewed all persons involved and learned the following:

Arresting Officer Huple said he remembered Rogers "making some off-the-cuff statement" about still loving his wife and whether he could "take it" but did not think too much about it because he hears things like that quite often. He did not tell Booking Officer Stanton about this.

Officer Stanton did tell Officer Williams about Rogers' statement about his previous attempted overdose.

Jail policy and procedure did not outline any definite instructions on identifying and managing potentially suicidal offenders.

Case Study—Administrative Review (continued)

Even though all Wilson County officers completed entrance training at the academy, the county did not require any refresher training in suicide prevention. There was no in-service training on suicide prevention.

A prior suicide hanging death occurred at the jail three years ago, involving use of the air vent, but no changes were made to prevent further suicides.

A prior suicide hanging death occurred at the jail three years ago.

QUESTIONS

An administrative review was held the day after Rogers' suicide, with Sheriff Evans stating, "This is our second suicide death. I want you folks to be open and frank. What did we miss? How do we prevent another one?" Sheriff Evans invited Dr. Johnson, Director of the Wilson County Mental Health Clinic, to participate.

Answer Sheriff Evans's questions below. Then compare your answers with the ones generated during the review, which can be found under number 7 in the answer key.

_____

_____

_____

_____

_____

_____

_____

_____

_____

This chapter examined the administrative review. It also explained the importance of dealing openly with staff feelings about the suicide.

1. List at least three issues that are discussed in the administrative review.

  • Administration and all involved staff should conduct a thorough evaluation of the facts and circumstances surrounding a completed (or an attempted) suicide

  • Everyone involved in a suicide (or attempted suicide) should participate in the administrative review and discuss:

    — Missed signs and symptoms

    — Policies and procedures

    — Training and re-training

    — Mental health and medical staff input

    — Staff concerns, including inadequate communications

2. List at least three items that should be included in the report about the administrative review.

  • Names and titles of staff in attendance

  • Description of:

    — The administrative review (process)

    — The circumstances of the incident

    — What, if anything, could have been done to prevent the completed suicide from having occurred

    — What changes in current policies and procedures, if any, are necessary to reduce the likelihood of such a completed suicide occurring again

3. Identify at least two positive outcomes of an administrative review.

  • It helps staff prevent the next attempted or completed suicide.

  • It helps staff and the facility avoid liability.

  • It gives staff an opportunity to express their feelings.

  • It provides an opportunity to modify policies and procedures, and update the suicide prevention plan.

  • After a completed suicide, some correctional workers blame themselves for "not having done better." They may suffer from severe guilt feelings that remain for years. Some of them might even resign after the suicide because of the way they feel.

  If you undergo such a difficult period as a correctional worker, remind yourself of this crucial fact: even experienced psychiatrists have admitted that they misjudged suicide victims and, thus, were not able to predict a suicide.

Answer Key—Administrative Review and Follow-up Support for Staff

1. An administrative review is a thorough evaluation of the facts and circumstances surrounding a completed (or an attempted) suicide.

2. **True**. Correctional workers need to express their feelings about an attempted or completed suicide, and administrators need to recognize those feelings. This professional, unemotional "venting" may be all that is necessary to ward off any long-term negative effects.

3. The purpose of the administrative review is to prevent the next attempted or completed suicide.

4. Things that should be included in the report about the administrative review are: (choose three)

   - The administrative review (process)

   - The circumstances of the incident

   - What, if anything, could have been done to prevent the completed suicide from having occurred

   - What changes in current policies and procedures, if any, are necessary to reduce the likelihood of such a completed suicide occurring again

5. Participants in the administrative review should discuss:

   - Missed signs and symptoms

   - Jail policy and procedures

   - Training and re-training

   - Mental health and medical staff input

   - Staff concerns, including inadequate communication

6. You can avoid miscommunication with mental/medical staff about a suicidal offender by telling them about new signs/symptoms of suicidal behavior that you observe.

7. Several staff collectively cited these high suicide risk factors:

   - Prior suicide attempt

   - Intoxicated at arrest

   - History of chemical dependency

   - Rejection by a loved one

   - "I don't think I can take it"—possible death-related statement, at least reflecting hopelessness

   - The Jail Captain said that suicide prevention training should be done. He said it was his understanding that entrance training at the academy is only an *overview*. To make suicide prevention *operational*, it must be done in-house, with refresher training at least every two years.

   - The arresting officer said, "On second thought, I should have told Stanton about that statement Rogers made en route to the jail."

- Jail Officer Williams: "I didn't have the time to watch Rogers closely. I was alone. I should have put him in cell Number One next to the officer post and asked the trustee to keep an eye on him until he went to sleep."

- Dr. Johnson: "Even if an arrestee is only intoxicated, he should be observed very closely because he may have a serious *medical* problem that has the same symptoms as intoxication. Also, intoxication alone is a major 'red flag' sign of suicide risk, because it causes depression when the person sobers up."

- Sheriff Evans: "My gosh! We need to get you to do some suicide prevention training, Dr. Johnson."

- Officer Stanton: "Since Roberts committed suicide two years ago also by tying the noose to the air vent, can't we do something about closing off those wide openings between the fins or cross pieces in at least one or two cells?"

- Sheriff: "I'll call the state jail inspector and see what he suggests we do."

  "Equally important, I'm going to submit another request to the County Board for a second day and evening jail officer. One can't do it alone, particularly without having either closed-circuit TV or audio monitoring."

- Dr. Johnson: "Do you have a written policy and defined procedures to guide staff on handling potentially suicidal offenders? Even though I do the training, the written procedures are very important as reminders of what to do because people can't remember everything from the training."

- Sheriff Evans: "Please give me a rough draft of the suggested procedures that we can put into the policy and procedure manual."

- Officer Williams said that he saw a "911 Rescue Tool" advertised in the State Police Journal and recommended that one be purchased because there was a delay in cutting Rogers down.

- Sheriff Evans: "I am changing our policy on 'Never enter a cell without backup' for any suicide attempt that might occur again. I learned that some jails give the jailer authority to use their judgment on such a matter, including using the trustee to help them get the man down."

Controversial Approaches to Preventing Suicides in Custody

Objectives

At the end of this chapter, you will be able to:

1. Describe at least six controversial methods to prevent suicides in custody, and explain why they are controversial.

2. Describe two alternative methods to prevent suicides in custody.

Introduction

Experts believe that some methods used by correctional agencies for preventing suicides are controversial and, sometimes, dangerous. Agencies often say they use these particular methods because they have "no other alternatives" or because "that's all [they] can afford to do." Should agencies use these methods if they can document that "this is the best that we can do"? That is ultimately for the courts to decide in the future. In the meantime, you should be familiar with the pros and cons of these methods because your facility may be using them.

Some agencies try to be creative in preventing suicides in custody. They use alternative methods that avoid many of the problems of the controversial methods. You also should be familiar with these alternatives for the same reason.

This chapter will discuss the pros and cons of using controversial methods to prevent suicides in custody. It also will discuss the creative or alternative methods.

Controversial Approaches to Preventing Suicides in Custody

Below are various controversial methods used by facilities to prevent suicides in custody. If you are required by policy to use one or more of these methods, discuss your concerns with your supervisor.

Signing "No Suicide" Contracts with Suicidal Offenders

Some facilities sign formal contracts with suicidal offenders. According to these contracts, the offenders agree not to commit suicide if mental health services are forthcoming.

These facilities have reported success with this method. Mental health workers stress that this approach gets across to the offender that "someone does care"—a major factor in preventing suicides. They believe the contract is an important part of a complete treatment plan. However, this method poses one danger. A facility may not be able to provide services at the crucial **time**. Or, at least when the offenders' perceive the crucial time to be.

Thus, most attorneys recommend that facilities not sign such *formal* contracts with suicidal offenders.

Q

QUESTIONS

What dangers do "no suicide" contracts pose?

_____

_____

_____

(1)

Stripping Suicidal Offenders Naked

Some facilities strip suicidal offenders naked so that they cannot hang themselves with their own clothes. The offenders are then placed in single cells/rooms.

Most suicide prevention experts agree that this practice merely adds to the suicidal offenders' degradation and worsens their depression.

In addition, experience has shown that stripped offenders can still kill themselves in "imaginative ways." For example, the offenders stuff both their nostrils and throat with toilet paper or bedclothing, passing out within 30 seconds, and totally asphyxiating themselves in 12–15 minutes.

More suitable approaches are:

- Maintaining constant supervision through trained staff and/or trained volunteers, who may be civilians or non-predatory offenders.

- Placing suicidal offenders in suicide-resistant rooms with close staff supervision.

- Placing suicidal offenders with two or more carefully selected, trained, and trusted offenders, and providing staff supervision every ten to 15 minutes.

Note: In Oregon, a U.S. District Court judge ordered jail officers to stop stripping suicidal inmates naked and to conduct two-minute watches instead.

Most suicide prevention experts agree that this practice merely adds to the suicidal offenders' degradation and worsens their depression

QUESTIONS

What is the problem with stripping suicidal offenders naked?

_____

_____

(7)

What is an alternative to this approach?

_____

_____

(9)

Controversial Approaches to Preventing Suicides in Custody (continued)

Relying Mainly on Closed Circuit Television (CCTV) to Monitor Suicidal Offenders

Some facilities rely mainly on CCTV to monitor suicidal offenders. This method, however, poses several problems. It doesn't provide human interaction and is impersonal. Suicidal offenders usually need to know that someone cares about them.

CCTV also is often fuzzy, and the system often breaks down. Moreover, a correctional worker may be distracted by other duties, or may become "hypnotized" by the monitor. In one case, for example, an offender died even though a camera had been "photographing" him for 85 minutes. The correctional officer had "monitor hypnosis" and did not see what he was looking at. Thus, correctional workers should not watch monitors for a full shift. In addition, they should not watch for more than *one hour* without a break; a five-minute break every half-hour is recom-

mended. Some facilities are aware of the "hypnosis" reaction and limit how long their workers can watch monitors.

A question usually arises about CCTV from both those inside and outside of corrections: Is CCTV monitoring of a suicidal offender an invasion of privacy?

NO! Courts do not consider CCTV monitoring of an offender an invasion of privacy if staff have assessed the offender as a potential suicide victim. **Life-safety** is more important than privacy. In fact, a court could rule against a facility for failure to use CCTV in such a situation.

CCTV monitoring of **all** offenders, however, might be considered an invasion of privacy by the courts.

In sum, CCTV—when it is working—can be relied upon only as a **supplement** to personal observation.

Q

QUESTIONS

List two problems with relying mainly on CCTV to monitor suicidal offenders.

* _____

* _____

(3)

True/ False   Courts do not consider CCTV monitoring of a suicidal offender an invasion of privacy.

(5)

True/False   CCTV should be used only as a supplement to human or personal supervision.

(13)

Using Numerical Scales to Rate Offenders on their Suicide Risk

Some facilities rank individuals on a numerical scale, according to their level of suicide risk. (See Chapter 6, "Assessing Suicidal Risk: Special Aspects of Health Clearance and Receiving Screening.") Most suicide prevention experts believe, however, that no one is skillful enough to determine such levels of risk.

Thus, you must consider some offenders as high-risk suicide candidates even if they have only one trait on the rating sheet. For example, all offenders "under the influence" upon admission require suicide monitoring—whether or not they have other traits listed on the rating sheet. The same holds true for someone who threatens to kill himself.

An offender with _____ trait on a rating sheet might be a _____ suicide candidate.

(11)

QUESTIONS

Controversial Approaches to Preventing Suicides in Custody (continued)

Using a "Paper Profile" as the Most Important Suicide Predictor

Some facilities rely mainly on a "paper profile (study)" to identify potentially suicidal offenders. Suicide prevention experts agree, however, that there is no "typical" suicide. Thus, facilities should use national, regional, or local suicide profiles (studies of common suicide traits) to sensitize correctional workers to the most important suicide traits—rather than viewing these studies as being the most important suicide predictor.

From a national perspective, the following signs and symptoms or traits should be given serious consideration in assessing suicide risk.

- History of mental illness, particularly depression

- Chemical dependency history

- First time incarcerated

- "Under the influence" at the time of arrest

- Prior suicide attempt(s), thoughts

- Significant loss, e.g., divorce, job, finances

- Unusual agitation

- Significant mood and/or behavior changes

Indeed, correctional workers should be trained to place more importance on what is observed at these four stages of the criminal justice system (e.g., comments and "body language" indicating suicidal behavior):

- Arrest

- Transportation

- Booking

- Confinement

Facilities should use profiles to help sensitize correctional workers to the most important suicide traits.

True/False   Suicide profiles should be used as the most important suicide predictor.

QUESTIONS

(8)

Controversial Approaches to
Preventing Suicides in Custody (continued)

Having a Policy that Says: "Never Enter a Cell or Room Without Backup"

Some facilities have a policy that prohibits their workers from entering a cell or room without backup. Many suicide prevention experts believe this policy is too rigid and recommend a more flexible one. In particular, these experts believe workers should be allowed to use their own judgment on whether to enter a cell or room alone.

How does the lone worker handle a suicide victim? The basic steps include: alerting control to the emergency, locking offenders down, selecting one or two offenders to assist in responding to the suicide victim, and immediately entering the cell or room. If trouble arises, backup support should arrive in time to provide assistance. The order of these steps may vary depending on the facility. You should check with your supervisor, therefore, to see how your facility handles this situation.

If the lone worker stands idly by waiting for several minutes for backup, the suicide victim may die. A one- or two-minute delay in cutting a victim down and/or initiating CPR can make the difference between life, death, or brain damage. In addition, the facility probably will lose a lawsuit related to the suicide.

QUESTIONS

True/False You should alert control before entering a cell or room alone.

(4)

True/False Many suicide prevention experts recommend that facilities have a policy that prohibits workers from entering a cell or room without backup.

(16)

Controversial Approaches to Preventing Suicides in Custody (continued)

Protecting the Scene of the Crime Before Cutting Down a Hanging Victim

In some facilities, correctional workers have concentrated on protecting the scene of the crime before cutting down a hanging victim. Such a practice can result in death. In addition, the courts probably will render a negative ruling for failure to cut down a hanging victim immediately. In one facility, the officers waited until the administrator was informed of the hanging. Upon his arrival, photographs were taken and the body was left hanging until the coroner arrived and viewed it.

You must remember at all times that **preserving life comes before preserving evidence**.

Believing a Victim is Dead upon Finding No Vital Signs

Tragically, in some facilities, offenders die in their suicide attempts because correctional workers do not perform first aid. They look for vital signs and, finding none, assume that the victim is dead.

Only a physician or other qualified professional(s), as designated by state law, can pronounce a person dead. Until such time, correctional workers should *start* and *continue* cardiopulmonary resuscitation (CPR).

Q

QUESTIONS

Preserving _____ comes before preserving _____.

(2)

If an offender has no vital signs, you should

_____

_____

_____

(12)

Having a Policy that Prohibits Correctional Workers from Talking with Offenders

A few facilities have written policies that prohibit their correctional workers from talking with offenders. These policies usually state that workers should "just do their job." Most suicide prevention experts agree that such policies are harmful. They believe that correctional workers should be able to talk with offenders. *And, that positive human interaction and communication provides the most effective suicide prevention.*

Tragic scenarios have occurred in facilities where correctional workers were conditioned to avoid talking with offenders. The informer or "snitch system" that naturally arises is a dangerous way to keep informed about "what is going on." One prison had a major riot over this concept. Many offenders lost their lives and many officers were injured.

Note: Many correctional workers who are allowed to talk with offenders often ask a question similar to this one: "Should I take the ninth 'wolf cry' of a suicidal offender as seriously as the first one?" The answer is, "Yes." You must take *all* threats of suicide seriously. Offenders have committed suicide because their "manipulation" or attention-getting behavior was not taken seriously. In addition, facilities have been held liable in lawsuits related to such incidents.

QUESTIONS

True/False   You must take all suicide threats seriously, including the ninth "wolf cry."

(14)

True/False   Most suicide experts agree that it doesn't matter whether correctional workers talk with offenders.

(6)

Alternative Approaches to Preventing Suicides in Custody

Using Volunteers and Offenders to Monitor Suicidal Offenders

Some facilities use volunteers, and selected and trained offenders to monitor suicidal offenders. While this practice is not controversial with most suicide prevention experts, it is controversial with some correctional administrators. They refuse to use volunteers because:

- "They are hard to recruit."

- "You cannot always count on them."

- "Our facility is afraid of the liability issue."

Experience has shown, however, that such programs are successful when supported by top administration.

In some facilities, carefully selected, trained, and supervised volunteers do an effective job of monitoring potentially suicidal offenders. Service groups screen and supervise their members who, in turn, assist facilities during suicide watches. Some jurisdictions even legally define volunteers as staff to prevent liability.

Volunteers should be trained by the facility before they begin to provide their service. This training should be documented and signed by the trainer and volunteers, the same as for staff.

Volunteers should be treated like staff in all aspects except pay. This means that they should be hired, trained, and supervised like staff. Volunteers should abide by the confidentiality principle. If they don't perform reasonably, they need to be released from service, the same as staff.

These individuals usually enrich the overall program. For example, volunteers often ask many good questions and provide many new ideas. Offenders say they like and respect volunteers "because they are not paid" and "we know they care." Experience has shown that better staff-offender relationships exist when volunteers are used.

QUESTIONS

Why do some correctional experts refuse to use volunteers to monitor suicidal offenders?

_____

_____

_____

(15)

Using the Companion System

Various correctional facilities are successfully selecting, training, and supervising offenders for suicide watches. Mental hospitals have used this approach successfully for several decades.

So far, one facility has been sued over using the approach and it is readily understandable why. Evidence at the jury trial showed that the sheriff provided inadequate training for the two officers working in the unit and did not require officers to visually observe offenders during hourly rounds. The two officers were either laying down and/or sleeping in the booth with lights out for the majority of their shift. They *did not supervise* the "inmate watchers." The jail's suicide prevention policies were grossly inadequate and the cell was inappropriate for housing suicidal inmates. A negotiated settlement of approximately $230,000 occurred. [*Natriello v. Flynn*, 837 F. Supp. 17(D. Mass. 1993) 26 Atla L. Rep. 368 (Dec. 1993)]

Offender suicide watchers should not be in the same cell or room as the suicidal offender. They can sit in front, across the hall, or next door to the cell or room, viewing through a large panel. These watchers are given **no control** over the suicidal offender. Instead, they are trained to notify staff of any unusual behavior.

Experience has shown that in reasonably operated systems, offender watchers benefit treatment-wise from helping their peers.

Being helpers or companions improves their morale and self-esteem. In addition, the relationship between offenders and staff involved in the program improves. They usually have a sense of teamwork.

The Federal Bureau of Prisons developed its selected and trained "companion" system in 1982. Fifty of its prisons and detention centers use the concept extensively. The program's administrator of psychology services said that in his 14 years as administrator, the companion system "has had a spectacular record. We have never lost an inmate where the system was used."

In fact, the suicide death rate in the Bureau facilities decreased by over 40 percent during the first ten years of its formal suicide prevention program (1983–1992) compared to the pre-program suicide rate. The companion program is credited with having a major impact on the reduction of suicide deaths.

Supervisors of suicide prevention programs—in both the Federal Bureau of Prisons and the New York City Department of Corrections—stress that the use of selected and trained inmates to support observation of suicidal inmates has clearly resulted in a noticeable reduction in the negative impact of the inmate "code of silence." Many suicide risk cases are brought to the attention of staff by inmates. During the 15 years of using inmates for suicide watch, there has been no harassment in either system by inmates in the general population.

QUESTIONS

True/False   Offender suicide watchers are given control over suicidal offenders.

(10)

Summary

This chapter presented the pros and cons of using controversial approaches to preventing suicides in custody.

1. Describe at least six controversial methods to prevent suicides in custody, and explain why they are controversial.

    The various controversial approaches listed below were presented to raise your level of awareness of possible problem and resource areas. Some of them may need to be reviewed if your facility is developing new policies. Others are mentioned to alert you to be cautious about accepting or using them.

    - Signing "no suicide" formal contracts with suicidal offenders. A facility may not be able to provide services at the crucial time, or, at least when the offenders' perceive the crucial time to be. Thus, most attorneys recommend that facilities not sign such *formal* contracts with suicidal offenders.

    - Stripping suicidal offenders naked. This practice merely adds to the suicidal offenders' degradation and worsens their depression. In addition, experience has shown that "stripped" offenders can still kill themselves in "imaginative ways."

    - Relying mainly on closed circuit television (CCTV) to monitor suicidal offenders. This poses several problems. It doesn't provide human interaction and is impersonal. CCTV also is often fuzzy, and the system often breaks down. Moreover, a correctional worker may be distracted by other duties, or may become "hypnotized" by the monitor.

    - Relying heavily on numerical scales to rate offenders on their suicide risk. Most suicide prevention experts believe that no one is skillful enough to determine such levels of risk.

    - Using the "paper profile" as the most important suicide predictor. Experts agree that there is no "typical" suicide. Thus, facilities should use national, regional, or local suicide profiles (studies of common suicide traits) to sensitize correctional workers to the most important suicide traits—rather than viewing these studies as being the most important suicide predictor. Correctional workers should be trained to place more importance on what is observed at these four stages of the criminal justice system (e.g., comments and "body language" indicating suicidal behavior):

        — Arrest

        — Transportation

        — Booking

        — Confinement

    - Having a policy that says: "Never enter a cell or room without backup." Many suicide prevention experts believe this policy is too rigid and recommend a more flexible one. In particular, these experts believe workers should be allowed to use their own judgment on whether to enter a cell or room alone.

- Protecting the scene of the crime before cutting down a hanging victim. Such a practice can result in death. In addition, the courts probably will render a negative ruling for failure to cut down a hanging victim immediately. You must remember at all times that **preserving life comes before preserving evidence**.

- Believing a victim is dead upon finding no vital signs. Only a physician or other qualified professional(s), as designated by state law, can pronounce a person dead. Until such time, correctional workers should *start* and *continue* first aid and cardiopulmonary resuscitation (CPR).

- Having a policy that prohibits correctional workers from talking with offenders. Most suicide prevention experts agree that such a policy is harmful. They believe that correctional workers should be able to talk with offenders. And, that positive human interaction and communication provides the most effective suicide prevention.

2. Describe two alternative methods to prevent suicides in custody.

- Using selected, trained, and supervised volunteers and offenders to monitor suicidal offenders. Experience has shown that such programs are successful when supported by top administration.

Volunteers usually enrich the overall program. For example, they often ask many good questions and provide many new ideas. Offenders say they like and respect volunteers "because they are not paid" and "we know they care." Experience has shown that better staff-offender relationships exist when volunteers are used.

- Using the companion system.

Various correctional facilities are successfully selecting, training, and supervising offenders for suicide watches. Mental hospitals have used this approach successfully for several decades.

Offender suicide watchers should not be in the same cell or room as the suicidal offender. They can sit in front, across the hall, or next door to the cell or room, viewing through a large panel. These watchers are given no control over the suicidal offender. Instead, they are trained to notify staff of any unusual behavior.

Experience has shown that in reasonably operated systems, offender watchers benefit treatment-wise from helping their peers. Being helpers or companions improves their morale and self-esteem. In addition, the relationship between offenders and staff involved in the program improves. They usually have a sense of teamwork.

Answer Key—Controversial Approaches to Preventing Suicides in Custody

1. "No suicide" contracts pose one danger. A facility may not be able to provide services at the crucial time, or, at least when the offenders perceive the crucial time to be.

2. Preserving **life** comes before preserving **evidence**.

3. Problems with relying mainly on CCTV to monitor suicidal offenders are: (choose two)
    - CCTV is often fuzzy
    - The system often breaks down
    - A correctional worker may be distracted by other duties
    - A correctional worker may be "hypnotized" by the monitor
    - It is impersonal

4. **True**. You should alert control before entering a cell or room alone.

5. **True**. Courts do not consider CCTV monitoring of a suicidal offender an invasion of privacy.

6. **False**. Most suicide experts *agree* that *correctional workers should talk with offenders*.

7. The practice of stripping suicidal offenders naked merely adds to their degradation and worsens their depression.

8. **False**. Suicide profiles should be used *to sensitize correctional workers to the most important suicide traits*—rather than used as the most important suicide predictor.

9. An alternate—and more suitable—method to stripping suicidal offenders naked is: (choose one)
    - Maintaining constant supervision through trained staff and/or trained volunteers
    - Placing suicidal offenders in suicide-resistant rooms with close staff supervision
    - Placing suicidal offenders with two or more selected, trained, and trusted offenders, and providing staff supervision regularly

10. **False**. Offender suicide watchers are given **no control** over suicidal offenders. Instead, by pre-arrangement, watchers must notify staff of any unusual behavior.

11. An offender with **one** trait on a rating sheet might be a **high-risk** suicide candidate.

12. If an offender has no vital signs, you should start and continue cardiopulmonary resuscitation (CPR) until qualified health personnel arrive.

13. **True**. CCTV should be used only as a supplement to human or personal supervision.

14. **True**. You must take all suicide threats seriously, including *repeated* ones.

15. Some correctional experts refuse to use volunteers to monitor suicidal offenders because:

    • "They are hard to recruit."

    • "You cannot always count on them."

    • "Our facility is afraid of the liability issue."

16. **False**. Many suicide prevention experts believe a policy that says, "Never enter a cell or room without backup"
    is too rigid. They recommend a more flexible one. Indeed, they believe *trained* correctional workers should be
    allowed to use their own judgment on whether to enter a cell or room alone.

Conclusions About Preventing Suicides in Custody

Conclusions About Preventing Suicides in Custody

In order for a suicide prevention program to be effective, top administration must understand and support the philosophy and processes of suicide prevention.

Proactive administrators, effective supervisors, and properly selected and trained correctional, mental health, and medical staff are key suicide prevention factors.

When the above factors, which reflect recognized standards and practices, are in place, most suicides in custody will be prevented.

A *written plan* must exist for identifying and managing potentially suicidal offenders; this is required by recognized national and state standards, guidelines or rules, and court decisions. This plan should address:

Training—Both government direct service and contract personnel must be fully trained to carry out suicide identification and management processes.

Contract health services personnel, whose only experience has been with suicides in the community, need to be trained because the correctional environment presents new factors. Lack of training for these individuals has resulted in numerous suicide deaths in correctional settings in the past. The deaths could have been prevented had additional, special training been provided. Eight hours of training is recommended for previously untrained government staff, and at least four hours for contract medical/mental health personnel who have not worked with or in correctional facilities. Training should include the "Do's and Don'ts of Good Discipline, Custody, and Mental Health," which help to develop greater self-understanding by staff.

Refresher training every other year is crucial for correctional and health care staff. The same holds true for first aid/CPR training.

Identification/screening—The process starts with the arresting officer. Intake/admission screening, generally as part of overall health screening, is carried out by trained law enforcement and detention/correctional personnel or by health staff in large facilities. Referrals for medical and/or mental health services may be done at that time.

Communications—Life safety comes before confidentiality in suicide prevention. Some deaths have occurred because mental health personnel failed to alert correctional staff about offenders' potentially suicidal behavior learned during counseling sessions.

A *team* approach requires all direct service personnel to keep each other fully informed about an offender's suicide potential/status. The on-site correctional officer or juvenile careworker generally is the only person to pick up on new developments in the offender's life that may lead to a suicide attempt. It is crucial that this information be conveyed to the shift supervisor and/or mental health staff immediately.

Housing—Defined procedures for housing potentially suicidal offenders should contain these provisions:

Constant observation—line of sight supervision—if placed in a single, protrusion-free cell/room. If lack of staff prevents this, place the offender with two or more carefully selected and trained offenders and check him at least every ten minutes. At night, one or more trained offenders should monitor the suicidal offender because suicide attempts often occur when other offenders are sleeping. Low risk, not actively suicidal offenders are best housed in the general population and monitored every 10–15 minutes on a staggered basis.

Conclusions About Preventing Suicides in Custody (continued)

Monitoring/Supervision—In addition to following the provisions outlined under "Housing," staff must exercise extreme caution when the offender is away from his cell/room. Suicide attempts occur in bathrooms, stairwells, closets, and vacant rooms.

Moreover, staff must exercise caution in using CCTV and not rely heavily upon it. CCTV is at risk for breaking down and also causes "monitor hypnosis," which may result in a hanging offender being undetected.

Intervention—Human interaction by caring staff is the most important form of intervention. If a hanging attempt is in process, getting the person down immediately is crucial. If no vital signs exist, cardiopulmonary resuscitation must be started immediately and continued until qualified health personnel arrive. Correctional staff must have face masks to administer CPR, and the "911" tool for rescue efforts.

Notification and Reporting—Agency procedures should outline how key persons, including officials and family members, are to be notified for both attempted and completed suicides.

Review—Specific procedures for medical and administrative review should be outlined in the facility's policies and procedures. Administration should provide a safe atmosphere in which staff can openly discuss problem areas. Support and counseling referral must be given to staff who need it. The more caring the staff, the greater likelihood of the need for support and counseling.

The proactive administrator sees to it that one suicide attempt or completed suicide results in measures designed to prevent the next one. He or she is the key person to ensure a true *TEAM* approach for suicide prevention. There should be no "turf problems," or "street attitudes" that deter staff from pursuing a "we care" philosophy.

R E F E R E N C E S

American Correctional Association. *Certification Standards for Health Care Programs* (Laurel, MD, 1989).

_____. *Standards for Adult Correctional Institutions* (Laurel, MD, 1990).

_____. *Standards for Adult Local Detention Facilities* (College Park, MD, 1981 and 1991).

_____. *Standards for Juvenile Detention Facilities* (College Park, MD, 1983 and 1991).

_____. *Standards for Juvenile Training Schools* (College Park, MD, 1983 and 1991).

American Medical Association. *Standards for Health Services in Jails* (Chicago, 1981).

American Medical Association (in cooperation with the Department of Governmental Affairs, University of Wisconsin). *Training of Jailers in Receiving Screening and Health Education* (Chicago, IL: American Medical Association, March 1978).

Atlas, Randy. *Guidelines for Reducing the Liability for Inmate Suicide* (Miami: Atlas and Associates, 1986).

Camp, George M. and Camille Graham Camp. *The Corrections Yearbook* (South Salem, NY: Criminal Justice Institute, 1989).

Commission on Accreditation for Law Enforcement Agencies. *Standards for Law Enforcement: Agencies* (Fairfax, VA, May 1987).

The Correctional Service of Canada. *The Prevention of Suicide in Prison* (Ottawa, Canada: Communications Branch, January 1981).

Cripe, Claire A. *Legal Aspects of Corrections Management* (Gaithersburg, MD: Aspen Publishers, Inc., 1997).

Dubler, Nancy N., ed. *Standards for Health Services in Correctional Institutions* (Washington, DC: American Public Health Association, 1986).

Finnerty, John P. *Suicide Prevention in Correctional Facilities* (Suffolk, NY: Suffolk County Sheriff's Office, 1978).

Flaherty, Michael G. *An Assessment of the National Incidence of Juvenile Suicide In Adult Jails, Lockups and Juvenile Detention Centers* (Urbana-Champaign, IL: Community Research Forum, 1980).

Hayes, Lindsay and Joseph R. Rowan. *National Study of Jail Suicides: Seven Years Later.* (Alexandria, VA: National Center on Institutions and Alternatives, February 1988).

_____ and Barbara Kajdan. *And Darkness Closes In . . . A National Study of Jail Suicides* (Washington, DC: National Center on Institutions and Alternatives, October 1981).

Hopes, Bobbie, Ph.D. and Ruth Shaull. "Jail Suicide Prevention: Effective Programs Can Save Lives," *Corrections Today* (December 1986).

Miller, Rod, ed. "Prisoner Suicide—Prescriptions for Prevention," *Detention Reporter,* 33 (July 1986).

National Commission on Correctional Health Care. *Standards for Health Services in Jails* (Chicago, 1987, 1992 and 1996).

_____. *Standards for Health Services in Juvenile Confinement Facilities* (Chicago, 1984 and 1992).

193

References (continued)

_____. *Standards for Health Services in Prisons* (Chicago, 1987 and 1992).

National Sheriffs' Association. *The State of Our Nation's Jails* (Alexandria, VA, 1980).

New York State Commission of Correction, State Office of Mental Health, Ulster County Community Mental Health Services. *The Officers' Handbook* (Albany, NY, March 1986).

_____. *Suicide Prevention and Crisis Intervention in County Jails and Police Lockups* (Albany, NY, March 1986).

North Dakota Combined Law Enforcement Council. "Suicidal Behavior in Jails," *North Dakota Correctional Officers Training Manual, Part II* (Bismarck, ND, June 1981).

Rowan, Joseph R. *Almost All Suicides in Jails and Lockups Can be Prevented If . . .* (monograph) (Roseville, MN: Juvenile and Criminal Justice International, Inc., 1984).

_____. "Beware the Halo Effect of Mental Health Personnel When They Say 'Not Suicidal.' Recommended: A National Policy Change," *American Jails* (January- February 1991).

_____. "Design, Equipment, Construction and Other Blunders in Detention and Correctional Facilities," *American Jails* (July-August 1990).

_____. "Detecting Potential Suicide Victims," *CORHEALTH* (February-April 1991).

_____. "Health Care in Jails and Prisons," *Encyclopedia of Social Work*, 19th Edition (Washington, DC: National Association of Social Workers, 1995).

_____. "Health Care Providers with 'Street Attitudes' Incur Lawsuits," *CORHEALTH* (March-May 1989).

_____. "Jail/Correctional Officers with 'Street Attitudes' Incur Lawsuits," *American Jails* (Spring 1989).

_____. "The Prevention of Suicide in Custody," *The Correctional Psychologist* (April 1996).

_____. "Sample Policy and Defined Procedures for Decelerating or Removing an Inmate from Suicide Watch," *Jail Suicide Update* (Winter 1990).

_____. "Suicide," *Encyclopedia of American Prisons* (New York: Garland Publishing, Inc., 1996). (Marilyn D. McShane and Frank P. Williams, III, eds.).

_____. "Suicide Prevention: Debunking the 'Experts,'" *American Jails* (November- December 1994).

_____. and Lindsay M. Hayes. *Training Curriculum on Suicide Detection and Prevention in Jails and Lockups* (Alexandria, VA: National Center on Institutions and Alternatives, February 1988 and March 1995).

U.S. Department of Justice. "The 1983 Census," *Bureau of Justice Statistics Bulletin* (Washington, DC, November 1984).

Notes

Notes

Notes

Notes

Notes

Notes